The Grass Library

The Grass Library

ESSAYS

David G. Brooks

Ashland
Creek
Press

The Grass Library

Essays by David G. Brooks

Published by Ashland Creek Press

Ashland, Oregon

www.ashlandcreekpress.com

First published in Australia by Brandl & Schlesinger in 2019

www.brandl.com.au

ISBN 978-1-61822-090-5

Library of Congress Control Number: 2020932469

Cover design by Matt Smith.

for Charlie, Henry, Jonathan, Jason,
and Orpheus Pumpkin

Hinterlands

It was one hot, rainy summer night at dinner in the small rented house at Govetts Leap, covered with wisteria, surrounded by funnel-web and black house spiders, that T. put her fork down and said, "I can't do this anymore."

She was referring to the curry, thank goodness, and not to our relationship, though it took a few panicked seconds to work that out. It's true the curry, a packet *palak gosht* from the Indian grocery in Concord, was rather ordinary. But she didn't mean curry per se; she meant meat. "I can't do it, to animals," she said, with tears running down her face—this from someone who hardly ever cries—as if she'd just realized something devastating. "We're turning vegetarian." As simple as that. And something clanged into place, like a great door shutting, or opening. I felt cruel suddenly, exposed, deeply wrong. I suppose that's what had just happened to her.

First shock aside, it wasn't so hard. I'd had periods as a vegetarian long before I met her, and we'd already had to make so many other changes in our lives in order just to be together that this one seemed easy. It's amazing what kind of resolve that can give you, just being together, resolve and a kind of clarity, although my resolve wasn't quite so clear when scarcely a week later I found myself responding to a further dinner-time declaration, and agreeing to become vegan. I hardly knew what a vegan was. I remembered something about no onions, no garlic, no salt. "No," she said, "it's not that extreme; it's just no meat, no eggs, no dairy. Nothing that's come from an animal. That means fish," she said, as if I hadn't guessed that already, "and oysters."

My collection of oyster knives ...

I found it hard at first to give up cheese and for a while was guilty of an occasional backslide, but even these ceased after a month or two—you realize how inconsistent you're being, and how childish—and we came to see it not so much as a giving-up of things as entering a new world of taste. There was, too, an unexpected pleasure—relief—in the thought that just by *not* doing something we were saving lives. You don't realize the guilt you've been suppressing until you no longer feel it. "Now I can look at you in peace," writes Kafka: "I don't eat you anymore."

But this book isn't about veganism, or guilt. If I'd permitted myself a nice, eighteenth-century subtitle it might have been *An Account of Three Years of Philosophical and Un-Philosophical Transactions with Animals in the Blue Mountains of New South Wales*, but ultimately and more simply it's about discovery and wonder: wonder, and wondering. Slipping into a flow of things—of *being*—that all your life, without realizing it, you've been holding back from. The only point in mentioning those things—and that Govetts Leap period—is that they were a beginning, the beginning of a beginning. It wasn't long before we were signing petitions about various animal matters, then attending rallies against live export—those death ships—or the use of battery cages. Indeed it was at a rally against the latter that, finding myself, a senior academic, crammed into a cage in Martin Place, wearing a chicken mask—watching the vice chancellor of my university walk by, brushing aside some of my fellow protesters in the same cavalier way I might have used myself a year or so before—that I realized just how much my life had changed.

It wasn't long, too, before we moved from our temporary mountain home to a little rental house in Glebe, in the inner city, close to the university, and a few weeks later adopted Charlie. In fact he was with us, on a lead, that time in Martin Place. He's a nervous dog, but crowds have never been his problem. Even now, at ten, after seven years in the mountains, he seems never so happy as when, on one of our occasional trips down to the city, he can wander along King Street or Glebe Point Road.

And then, after a long wait, the means at last coming our way, we began to think of putting down a deposit on a house of our own. We placed a bid for a tiny house on Darghan Street, three doors down from the one we were renting, although in truth, as I walked away from the real estate agency, I felt anything but elated. Another mortgage, and—Sydney being one of the most expensive cities on the planet—a huge one at that. Money worries until death. For the sake of a trendy address and a house near the university. What were we doing?

T. was clearly feeling the same. How else to explain—this is something you need to know about T., that when she comes up with an "idea" it's often tantamount to a decision already made—that, not more than a block or two from depositing our bid for an extremely expensive inner-city shoebox, she said, "Or there's the mountains … " and began to list some of the properties and prices she'd been finding online while I'd been lecturing that morning. We left it in the hands of fate, breathed a huge sigh of relief when our seemingly astronomical bid for the shoebox was unsuccessful (way too low) and began, in early autumn, to look for a house in the mountains.

We found one, in a town at the top, one hundred kilometers from the city. A brick house on Railway Parade, a wide street up front, a leafy gully in the back, plenty of room to grow vegetables, a couple of majestic Blue Mountains ash trees, a study for each of us, and a large art deco living room with a huge Persian rug the vendors said they'd throw in for free, for Charlie. The westerly wind blasted the kitchen at the back and no door snakes or window seals could keep it out; the much-vaunted gas central heating struggled to warm the place; there were blackouts during the dramatic summer and winter storms, funnel-web spiders in the garden (again), black house spiders in the basement; mowing the steep back yard was a dangerous and torturous exercise; and from the day-care center next door the delighted shrieking of children could make it hard to hear yourself think, but it was a four-minute walk from the train, a six-minute walk from the center of town, a two-block drive from the highway, and compared with the little place in the city it seemed like a palace. I could take my books and papers out of storage; I could put pictures on the walls rather than pile them under the bed. On the first morning waking there I heard whipbirds and kookaburras and currawongs and thought I was in paradise.

For the first year, however, addicted to carbon monoxide and anxiety, we kept renting in Sydney and came up only on weekends, still in two minds. Certainly the idea of commuting to work two hours each way on a train, or an hour and a half each way driving, didn't appeal to me. But when our city landlady developed cancer and needed the little inner-city house to be near the hospital for treatment we took it as a sign and moved up to the mountains permanently, or so we thought. After a year and a half T. was restless and figured it was because she was missing the city, and that Charlie might be missing it, too. Doing our sums it seemed we might just be able to go back to the previous weeks-in-the-city/weekends-in-the-mountains arrangement, if we could manage to find a city rental cheap enough.

Our previous place was no longer available—I don't know how things had panned out for the landlady, but there were other people now living in it—and so we looked in Balmain, the old workers' suburb on a peninsula on the southern shore of the harbor, now rapidly yuppifying. We joked that the house we found, after weeks of looking, was the smallest in Australia, and surely it would have come close. In dreams I would hold it in the palm of my hand. But it had, for T., a miniscule studio at the bottom of its tiny garden, and a large patio umbrella to cover almost all the rest, and in that summer's heat wave it was actually a delightful place to write or, shoving the books aside on the rickety outdoor table, have a small, cramped dinner with friends. Internet reception was lousy, and the poisoned soil struggled to produce seven cherry tomatoes and a five-centimeter, semi-dried baby eggplant, but you could smell the sea and at night, sometimes, catch the haunting sound of a ship's horn.

As the weather cooled, however, we found ourselves increasingly miserable. The wind blasted the tiny harbor-side park we'd tried to persuade ourselves Charlie was enjoying, and the relentless damp wormed into our minds. We pleaded our way out of the contract, went back to the mountains, and felt we'd taught ourselves a lesson. But still there was restlessness. We didn't quite know what it was until a year later when, sick of the joyful screaming from the day-care center, finding it harder and harder to concentrate on her work, and less and less inclined to return the rubber balls over the fence before Charlie got his teeth into and deflated them, T. found, online (again), a tiny farm at the edge of town.

It wasn't just that. In fact two things were coming together. On health grounds I'd decided to leave the university, if I could. A bad leg I'd had for decades—misdiagnosed—had recently been joined by a bad hand and, seeing a neurologist at last (my powers of denial are impressive), I'd been told I had MS, the perfect writer's disease, I sometimes joke, since the letters also designate "manuscript." Then, twelve months later, a family curse catching up with me, I also had a heart attack, "silent," as in completely painless, but a stark wake-up call nevertheless. Perhaps it was time. The university, once a place of thought, freedom, and light, had begun to seem a grim factory run by automatons, turning some of my nice, carp-like colleagues into piranhas (my last animal metaphor there, if I can help it: see it as a farewell).

We called the agent and arranged an inspection. It was love at first sight. Two sloping acres. At the top, on the cleared part—the old farm—a weatherboard house with a deck, a veranda, and a high kitchen window with a sweeping view over what I've come to call the Hidden Valley, and, just below, a two-room log cabin, empty but for a pot-bellied stove and a yellow, out-of-tune piano, that I could turn into a library. There were large water tanks, a vegetable garden, a farm shed attached to the bottom of the cabin, horseshoes nailed to its uprights, an old chicken coop just below it, an old swimming pool (but how often would *that* get used, up here in the mountains?), and, at the bottom, over a rusted, tumbling fence, a second acre of protected bush, "hanging" swamp, a creek. There was thick bush, too, all along one side, an untouched property, also protected. Huge peppermints and stringybarks, large tree ferns, a pair of black cockatoos flying high overhead. We finished the inspection by driving around to the bottom of the property, to get a better view of the swamp. It had been a gray day, but the sun had just broken through. Looking up, I gasped at a broad patch of bright emerald-green through the trees, realized with delight and wonder that it was grass just below the cabin.

It seemed too good to be true. We kept looking for the catch, became only the more uncertain when we couldn't find it. We'd have to buy it immediately, well before selling the house on Railway Parade, and that'd be tricky. We made three attempts to climb the lawyers' stairs to sign the contract.

After the second we went to see the farm again. Needing a few minutes to think, I walked down by myself to the rickety middle fence and stared into the trees, listening for I don't know what. Silence, and then, suddenly, a splash, as of some large animal bathing. What was it, a kangaroo? a swamp wallaby? A thrill went through me. It seemed a sign. I turned around, still thinking, and walked up to the cabin, was "inspecting" the tank there, my mind racing with ideas, when I heard a rasping croak above me. I looked up and saw a huge, glossy white cockatoo staring down from the guttering. He seemed to be asking me what I was waiting for.

It's one thing to move onto a little farm, however, and quite another to write about it. That—*this*—has a different beginning. The precise moment is lost in time, but I think it was while we were in the first inner-city rental house— the house we first brought Charlie into, where he'd shivered so much under the dining-table—that a vegan friend and I agreed, over the phone (he was in Western Australia), that animals had had a poor rap in Australian literature, and that perhaps we should write something about this, as a way of exposing animal cruelty more generally. A vague project, at first, but one which has grown and diversified. I think of this book as a part of it, one channel in its delta.

Eighteen months or so later, maybe sensing that our project was changing direction, this friend asked me to list some of the things I might want to write about. *The animal in philosophy*, I said (nothing like ambition!), and *problems about writing about animals in the first place*, because already I'd started to encounter these, the way the language itself seems stacked against them, conditioning us, subliminally, to keep up the cruelty—and then, I don't know, perhaps I was looking at Charlie as I spoke, wondering yet again where his trembling was coming from, *and Charlie*, outrageous as the idea seemed; *I'd like to try to write a biography of Charlie.*

Almost as soon as I got off the phone I began to see that last idea as untenable. A biography? Of a dog? Hadn't Virginia Woolf failed disastrously at just such a project?[1] But there's another part of me that sees such things as challenges. If something seems untenable then perhaps it's because it suits the status quo to have it seem so, and so is all the more reason one should attempt it. For a year or two, as I got started on some of the other essays, the idea kept coming back. At some point I began making entries in my notebook—some of them form the basis of the next two chapters—and then, in one of the first weeks on the little farm, sitting at my newly installed desk in the cabin, one of the five black cockatoos from the bushland next door staring from the lone peppermint at the southern fence, I started to write ("Poor Charlie," I began, going back, thinking of the previous year or two), and kept it up, a little each day, not knowing if anything would come of it. About Charlie. About dusk anxiety. About writing. Eventually about the boys. And straying into places I'd never really thought about before.

That was November 2012, our second month at the farm. We weren't far into the third—we'd as yet told no one about our refuge dream—before a friend called, to alert us to the plight of two sheep, asking if we could possibly give them a home. And within two days—I've said T. works quickly—they were with us, Jonathan and Henry-Lee. It had been forty-five years since I'd even touched a sheep, but by the time December was over they were wandering into the cabin, wandering into the tomato beds, wandering into the sentences, pointing out what a fool I'd been to ever think that I could write about Charlie alone, or write about animals (or writing, or literature) without them.

1   *Flush* (1933).

Charlie

Dusk Anxiety[2]

Poor Charlie. I think he suffers from dusk anxiety. Every night, while we're preparing dinner, sitting there in the kitchen, placing himself exactly between the two of us as if determined to trip us up, quivering. Not constantly. It comes in waves. But the waves are lengthening, and the calm intervals between them shortening, as if the quivering were just catching breath.

At first, when this quivering wasn't so bad, I thought he was putting on an act to get attention. They say the breed trembles anyway—the "pure" breed of fox terriers. He's a fox terrier cross—with what, we've never been able to work out (*Andalusian*, I used to tell people at Wentworth Park)—and I suppose he could have inherited this part of them. His right hind leg, too, has trembled, intermittently, since the operation[3], especially after he's been running. He stands there with Vinny or Maddy or Lucia, his park friends, waiting for the ball to be thrown, and his leg quivers like crazy. He'll quiver, too, when he's nervous or excited, in anticipation. Sometimes it's accompanied by a strange guttural panting.

2   Written at the little farm but about our time on Railway Parade.
3   Explained in the next chapter.

11

We once thought this was asthma—it still might be (or an allergy to hay)—but we've also realized it can be anticipation. He'll do it when we're down in Sydney, for example, taking a right turn from Parramatta Road on our way to see my daughter and her partner, which for him is to see Muppet and Ellie, his best dog friends from almost the beginning of his time with us.

But this trembling, now, is more pronounced. Every evening this summer, when, though it's still light outside, we've gone into the kitchen to prepare dinner. Could it be to do with food preparation? The chopping board? The sound of the cleaver on wood (although all we ever cleave is vegetables)? But why, if that is so, doesn't it happen at lunchtime, since we prepare food together then, too?

I think it's dusk anxiety. I took him onto the deck one evening to watch the sunset, and he was quivering there, too. I remembered Temple Grandin's cattle press, how holding a steer tightly will supposedly calm him down, and so for the first few nights, seeing it so much worse, I'd pick Charlie up—I do it often enough anyway, pick him up and stand him on my lap to watch T. as she prepares her part of the dinner—and hold him tightly against my chest, but while holding him tightly *constricts* the trembling, it doesn't stop it.

One night T., who'd been chopping vegetables while we watched, came over towards us, and I noticed that as soon as she started to approach he stopped quivering. But now I think that was just coincidence. She's said the same when she's been holding him, that as soon as *I've* turned to look at him he's stopped quivering. But further tests have thrown this into doubt. The one most consistent factor, it seems to me, is dusk itself.

Twilight. Half-and-half light. The time *between* things. They say dusk is the time when you can escape, slip through the crack between the world of day and the world of night. According to Yeats, Irish villagers not all that long ago would warn their children not to be out at twilight for fear of being taken by the Sidhe or "people of the mounds"—ghostly, romantic, bigger-than-life beings—and find oneself *spirited away* into the world of faery. (Fancy that: being led, through that crack, by a dog, a few sheep, some ducks, a rat, to find oneself, as once so long ago I dreamt I might, in a secret kingdom of grass.)

I'd forgotten about it, dusk anxiety, until I came upon mention of it a few months ago on the internet. I'd never known it had a name, but I recognized it immediately. I once had a friend who had it, though she, too, I think, wouldn't have known what to call it. Probably, back in the early 1980s, it hadn't yet been given its name. But every evening, for a while between 5 and 7 p.m.—its range varied with the seasons and the light—she'd become quiet and sad, for no reason she would ever explain. It came on as the light was fading and would leave once night set in. She'd even cry sometimes, and wanted to be left to do so. Sadness is okay, she'd say: people have to be allowed their sadness. She seemed to be saying it as much to herself as to me.

Does Charlie feel a particular sadness? I just don't know. Sometimes, as I watch him thinking, it seems to me I see a shadow cross over his features. We've even thought, on at least two occasions, that he's had a breakdown of sorts, or was in the midst of one. Now that I push myself to try to describe it (is the choice to write, in this regard, a choice to push?) I think that, yes, these breakdown moments could well have been plunges into depression. In T.'s study once, in that tiny house in Glebe, he was lying in his beanbag staring a long time at a blank wall, when suddenly he began to tremble and pant in anxiety, as if he'd seen a ghost there, or some frightening memory had just come to him, or he'd sensed something, far off on our horizons, that we had no idea about. That's another thing I've learnt, that dogs hear things, smell things, that we have no notion of.[4] We're annoyed when a dog raises his/her head and growls, or races outside to bark at nothing. It's hardly ever nothing.

But there. The quivering might have a name. Enough people must have experienced it to have called for one. Dusk anxiety.

There's a certain logic to it. It's not unusual to feel invigorated in the morning, optimistic about how much you're going to be able to get done in the hours ahead, only to find the energy and productivity wane as those hours pass. You look back and find you've only done a fraction of what you'd planned. Work finishes. You face the night. You can turn your back on a lot of domestic things during the day—problems, arguments, loneliness—but in the bus or car on the way home, in the dusk, you're preparing yourself to deal with them again. It's very likely a mood as old as human society—older. I wouldn't be surprised if, at some great distance behind us, but a part of us for so long it's almost hardwired into the brain, *genetic* knowledge, there wasn't a very real anxiety brought about by night as the time of greatest danger and vulnerability. When we went—go—back into the safety of the cave. When fires are lit to ward off marauding predators. When someone

---

4   "I don't know how many tiny muscles there are in a dog's nose," I wrote after a trip with Charlie. "I leant back to look at him in the car today when I felt his muzzle on my shoulder—I wasn't driving—and there it was, wet and healthy within inches of my eyes, every muscle, every nerve at work, a glistening, miraculous organ taking in, as it seemed to me, a thousand directions at a time, attuned to the briefest trace, the most fleeting scent as we sped along, no one, single aroma, as it seems to me that I get, albeit in succession, as I move through the world, but a teeming array, caught by a faculty that makes radar seem simple; alert, beyond imagining, attent, so in the moment that there is no time for past or future—almost enough to make me feel exiled from the world."

keeps watch, so that others aren't attacked in their sleep. A kind of *momentum* gets us over it, most of the time. Things have got you going through the day, you're distracted, and then suddenly it's night, and you've got through it. There are rituals—the gym, the drink after work—but if something *interrupts* them it can be very different. I know that if ever for some reason I fall asleep in the afternoon and wake at dusk, it can be bleak, disorienting, as if I've lost a thread.

But what of Charlie? What ancient thing is coming out of his bones, his muscles, the billions of neurons in *his* brain? Why might it be worse lately? Why, if it *is* there, isn't it causing his trembling constantly? What could it mean that it comes and goes? What could it be that, at last, after six years with us, has brought it on again (he used to tremble a lot when we first brought him home from the refuge)? Could some propensity have always been there, and something else, some particular stress upon one or another of the autoimmune systems, served as a trigger, weakening the defenses against it? If he gets depressed, let's say—if something *else* depresses him—could that depression let some older anxiety out? But what could *that* be? We impose so many wounds upon the animals we think of as our pets or companions; taking them away from their mothers so early—barely weaned, if that—is only the beginning.

※

A brief digression. When writing about animals there is always, it seems, an elephant in the room—or, rather, since one of the first things you realize when you start to write about animals is that it's paradoxical and self-defeating to draw lazily upon that vast horde of animal expressions in our language (*killing two birds with one stone; letting the cat out of the bag; an elephant in the room*) the principal effect of which is only to reinforce, subliminally, our ancient prejudices and barriers against them—there is always a *Human* in the room, a very large Human, towering over us, to whom most of us are trying very hard, and often very successfully, to seem oblivious. It has many faces, many voices, many idioms. We'll meet it over and again (notice I call it *it*, rather than *she* or *he*, much as we tend to speak of animals) if only in the process of trying to avoid it. And it'll be saying various things. As I wrote the previous paragraph, for example, it was accusing me, yet again, of *anthropomorphism*. Perhaps I should explain why I am not much bothered about that. To *anthropomorphize* is to treat animals as if they were in some way human. To speak of them, for example, as if they could experience "human" emotions, such as "love" or "grief" or "embarrassment." This is apparently a poor and unobjective way of conceiving. Science—for, although the proscription against anthropomorphism has spread through the "humanities" like a contagion, it's from scientific quarters that the accusation most often comes—would have us use instead such terms as "pair bonding," "separation anxiety," etc.

I've got a few objections to this, but I'll restrict myself to two. Firstly, the idea that we can view anything from some position of "objectivity" above or beyond the human is simply naïve. As Nietzsche said, we see all things through the human head and cannot remove that head. Merely to *think* is to anthropomorphize. Secondly—more importantly, as far as I am concerned—barbarity itself begins with the thought that we are so different from the creatures we live amongst that we cannot know or even hazard how they feel. This is not only a lie to ourselves, for in many cases in the experience of almost all of us, we *do* know how some animal or another feels (*at home* the scientist *knows* how his/her dog feels, and yet "officially," in the laboratory—this phenomenon is known as *doubling*[5]—has no idea), but, since what is called anthropomorphism is central to what we call empathy, and since empathy is fundamental to compassion, in the denial of anthropomorphism is that repression of empathy which is fundamental to the horrific abuse of animals which has always scarred this civilization (and almost every other civilization I can think of).

Writing about the animal is always fraught territory. Even the term *animal* itself can be seen as objectionable, a blanket term that the Human in the Room uses to keep "them" at a distance and preserve the myth of its (i.e., that Human's) essential difference. Certainly Derrida thinks this:

> I avoid speaking generally about animals. For me, there are not "animals." When one says "animals" one has already started ... to enclose the animal into a cage. ... [T]o say "animal," and put them all into one category ... is a very violent gesture.[6]

But here—and what else could be expected of a logos that has in effect shut out non-human animals for millennia?—is one of those instances where what we might call a human logic doesn't serve very well our attempts to think the animal. There's no doubt that, as an umbrella term, "the animal" is an

5   A term I take from Robert Jay Lifton's *The Nazi Doctors: Medical Killing and the Psychology of Genocide* (Basic Books, 1988), in which he outlines the psychological splitting which enabled medical staff in the death camps to deal with the work required of them. (Please note that, and some hideous experimentation upon animals notwithstanding, I am *not* drawing any comparison between scientists and workers in the death camps.)

6   Transcribed from a filmed interview. The point is made more extensively in *The Animal That Therefore I Am* (Fordham University Press, 2002), 31/2.

act of intellectual violence, as Derrida says, but if, as he seems to imply, one must then, instead of using "the animal," *list one by one all the species to which one may be referring,* one has, given the magnitude of the task, effectually silenced oneself. Throughout this book, therefore, the term "the animal" (or "animals") will continue to be used, albeit "under erasure" (another Derridean term), *so as not to erase.*

Have I drifted away from Charlie, his trembling and dusk anxiety, the house on Railway Parade, the little farm upon which we've eventually come to rest? I'm not sure I have. "Realize," Leonardo da Vinci is reported to have said, "that everything connects to everything else." There are days here in the mountains when a mist rolls in suddenly, a bright, eerie whiteness so thick that everything disappears, the house, the great trees, the sheep in their paddock scarcely a dozen meters away. It would be ridiculous to say that language is like that, that our realm of ideas is like that, but would it be so ridiculous to say that there is more mist about them—more of the world about us that is hidden from us, by them—than we know?

Hard Hands[7]

The last few days have been full of rain. It's nearly midsummer but it's a week since we've seen even a few minutes of sunshine. They attribute this to the La Niña effect, a warm current close to the coast and prevailing easterlies bringing huge amounts of moisture onto the land. It doesn't bother Sydney so much because it's a thousand meters lower, but here in the mountains we seem to have been living in permanent cloud. I've felt it keenly enough myself—today, at 4 p.m., when there was some sunshine at last, I almost ran out the back door to stand in it—and for Charlie it must be much worse. He lives for his walks and his time in the park, and although he's had time there every day, on most days lately it's been in the rain, which he enjoys no more than the rest of us, with none of his friends there to run about with, since their human companions seem to have thought the weather *fit for neither man nor dog*. He's hardly seen another dog all week. Enough to bring on a mild depression in most creatures, I'd think. His trembling, perhaps accordingly, has been worse. But he was, still, trembling before the rain set in. What *else* could there be?

7   The last summer on Railway Parade.

It's summer, as I've said, and we're not down in Sydney as often as we used to be during term time—particularly now my resignation's been accepted—so he's not seeing his city friends much at all: Ellie, Muppet, or the gang at Wentworth Park. It's six weeks since he's spent any real time with any of them. Could *that* explain the increased trembling? Loneliness? Isolation? Intensified by the rain? I think I've just convinced myself of it. But there could be other factors.

Before Christmas (how do I tell this, the human-companion way? or—risking anthropomorphism!—as I imagine Charlie might tell it?) an elderly friend of his died, which is to say (the human-companion way), a friend of ours, a human friend, who had had two dogs, had one of them "put down" ("euthanized," "put to sleep": killed) because he, the dog, had become incontinent, had arthritis, was clearly in pain. To do our friend justice, she'd thought about this for some time and was deeply reluctant, but eventually came to think it best. She *had* had *three* dogs, and in fact it had only been a few months since she'd had to make the same decision about another of them, the eldest. Charlie was part of all this, a witness, if not to the actual procedure then to each dog's passing. Neither of the older dogs was Charlie's special friend—in fact he was (still is) "in love," as we fondly and anthropomorphically put it, with the youngest, Chloë, a small black poodle (he has a particular affection for poodles)—but he'd come to know them, lain on their cushions, eaten from their bowls, shared their company when he visited.

Our friend on each occasion had brought the body home, to bury in her yard. The two surviving dogs hadn't witnessed the burial of the first. Our friend had kept them inside, hoping that to them it might seem just that she had gone out with the oldest dog and not come back with him. But is it better for them to know, or not? On the second occasion she'd let the poodle witness the burial—in fact had brought the body home with Chloë in the car. Would it be too much to think that, when Charlie visited the next day (our friend thought Chloë needed cheering), Chloë told him what had happened, and showed him the grave? Or that when they traveled in the car, on their way to the park, they were conscious of the dead dog's smell there, the death riding with them? Or that they'd suspected—known—all along what had happened to the first? Could some of Charlie's dusk anxiety, this wet summer, be grief or, if not grief, a sense of death, its proximity, its imminence? A kind of existential crisis, if you will,[8] for surely it's absurd to think that humans alone can experience such things.

It's true that these weren't his first experiences of death or abrupt departure—of what T., who is writing a thesis on animal grief, has called "the sudden disappearance of a proximal subject"—and indeed his first and most serious love, a brown poodle (again) named Sylvia (a neighbor of ours in Glebe), had literally disappeared overnight when her human companion moved away; but it was perhaps the first time he'd been so close to it. (And also perhaps not, for we can't know what he experienced in the eighteen months before we adopted him. We *do* know he'd come to the refuge from a municipal pound, where he'd been on death row. What had he experienced there? Disappearance after disappearance, I imagine. I had not, before this moment, thought of post-traumatic stress disorder, but perhaps I should. I do know, too—a tangent, but only a slight one—that a part of the sometimes disproportionate sadness I feel at funerals is

8   A possibility—to continue my backroom debate with some of our great philosophers—that flies in the face of Heidegger's rather ridiculous "Humans die; animals simply perish." See pages 97 and 99 below.

that one death—one grief—brings up others; that it's never singular, never contained.)[9]

❧

Try to write about a dog, I told myself—try to think yourself *in* or *towards*—and, as you do so, think about the process, *write* about writing about a dog. I think I had a breakthrough with Charlie—a breaking through something in myself, a breaking *through* myself—when I *got down to his level* (a phrase I am most unhappy with, since it implies—which I don't wish to do—that in some way he is a "lower" being). But he *is* a lower being, I almost hear him remark, with characteristic (imagined) irony, although in stature only, since he is scarcely fifty centimeters tall while I am well over three times that. When I lie down beside him, however, we are the same height. Indeed, if I'm on my back and don't raise my head he virtually towers over me (and has me at his mercy). I had hitherto approached him, that's to say, with "hard hands," as I'd approached all dogs before him. Not as hard as many, perhaps, but hard enough. I'd placed an imaginary barrier about myself, a shield. A dog might lick me, but only my hands—and in truth I discouraged it, found it distasteful. A dog might lie at my feet, keep me company that way as I

9   Reading this passage five years later, I remember, as clearly I did not when I first wrote it, that just before we met Charlie, considering adopting a "rescue" dog, we visited death row at a large municipal pound. Overwhelmed by the desperation and misery there, I think we left in horror. We human animals carry such freight with us; how could it be any different for non-human animals? Indeed, living as they do in an occupied world, directly or indirectly subject to human oppression, one can imagine that, for many, the freight would be considerable. Perhaps one of the reasons we've invented the mindless (memory-less, aspiration-less) animal is to put our own minds at rest.

read, but not sit on my lap (its anus? in touch with my jeans? hardly!). As to play, well, I could conceive of ball throwing, or playing Frisbee, but rolling around with a dog on the floor? in accidental or intentional contact with any and all parts of its body? Again, no way. Let alone letting "it" lick my face, my ears, or nuzzling its own with my nose, rubbing its cheek to my cheek.[10]

But the game changed—*being* (Being) changed—when I got down on my knees, metaphorically as well as physically; a sudden relaxation came about in us both. I developed what I now think of as *soft* hands, or at least soft*er*, the tension of difference, of separateness, in that respect substantially reduced, if not in fact gone.[11] My point here being that it's also a language matter, that a lot of our shield is language, and that as we attempt to get down on our knees we shouldn't be surprised if it (language) resists us and, far more often than we might imagine, we have to bend or break it, avoid or *write around* some rocklike, resistant lump in it.

Typing that, I'm suddenly reminded of yet another major impediment to writing the life of Charlie—or, indeed, of any animal. Perhaps it's *the* major impediment. I have only human lives to go by; a whole lifetime of being imprinted with what are understood to be the key forces and events in the lives of members of my own species. But can I transpose these to Charlie? Can I assume that love, for example, or death, *are* key events in his life? And if they are not, or if there are others quite different to the key events of a human life, how can I

10 "Its"? No dog—indeed hardly any animal (there are some exceptions?)—is an "it," but on the one hand I dislike the awkward "his/her" formulations and, on the other, preserving the "it" here would seem to reflect, linguistically, the distance I was keeping.

11 Am I saying that my shield is gone? Hardly. A work in progress. A constant work, in which progress is not easy and not always made.

come to know about them? Yet if I presume insurmountable difference, *un*knowability, then aren't I simply reimposing the repression on the animal-in-mind that has facilitated their age-old and terrible abuse at human hands? But perhaps even our fundamental unease in such situations may not be what we think it is. Perhaps, in a logos so stacked against non-human animals, a feeling of illogicality as we try to bring them to mind may be a sign that we are making progress.

꽃

I think the people at the refuge were surprised when we said we'd like to offer Charlie a home. He's a beautiful dog—was a beautiful pup—and a lot of people, seeing his picture on the website, had come in to meet him, but he was so lost in his anxiety, his nervousness, that I think they were all scared to take him on. When we took him for a walk around the neighborhood, as the refuge people suggested we should before we decided, he pulled at the lead so much we were afraid he'd injure his throat, so desperate did he seem to get away from that place, and maybe from us. But then there was a moment, back in the playpen with the other pups. He was in a corner, shivering. I knelt down and looked at him, and he looked up. The eyes of two creatures locking, just fleetingly. For me it was enough. As for T., well, I think she'd already decided. The more of a problem it seemed he might be, the more I think she was determined to solve it.[12]

We took him home, and for the first few days he hid under the dining table, trembling. We'd take him for walks—

12 T. adds a footnote here—something I didn't notice at the time—that when we first saw him, in the "display" pen, he was playing delightedly with (you guessed it) a poodle pup. Why on earth, she now asks, didn't we adopt them both?

awkward, since he pulled so much on the lead—and on the fourth or fifth day, frightened by a dog who rushed barking to a fence (and who later became one of his friends), he slipped his collar and ran out onto a busy road. A car hit him, but only a glancing blow, and he kept on running. By the time T. got to the other side (I was teaching a class) he was nowhere to be found. She called me, and I came as soon as I could. We searched all afternoon and into the early evening, until rain set in. We had a bleak dinner and, the rain getting heavier, sat an hour or so afterward, trying to work out what to do, hoping that he'd found a place somewhere out of the downpour. Then, at eleven, we heard a scratching at the door. He'd come back. I don't know what options he'd had, or where he'd been, but to us it was as if he'd made a decision.

Still he trembled. Not always, and sometimes he might go all day without doing so. To people who noticed and asked about it I'd say it was something about the breed, but in truth, as I've said, we just didn't know. It happened most pronouncedly after running. His right hind leg would tremble and he'd favor it, walk/skip home on three. As the months grew colder he'd favor it all the more, even at home. The trembling would begin in that leg and then spread through his entire body, rolling through him in spasms.

Was it arthritis? Could he be in pain? The vet x-rayed him, detected a congenital deformity. The ball-and-socket joint in that hip was more of a hook-and-socket. He'd been in great discomfort all this time. The vet's solution—and there seemed nothing else we could do—was to operate, to remove the hook in the hope that, since he was a small dog, the muscle might strengthen to the point where it could function without an actual bone connection to the hip. And it seems the vet was right: it took almost two years, but eventually Charlie was running on all four legs as if there'd never been a problem.

As to his life before all that—before us—it's anybody's

guess. Rescue dogs don't often come with biographies. All we can do is watch and play a kind of game of deduction. He's terrified by brooms: was he beaten with one? And has a strong affinity for young Chinese men. Was one particularly kind to him at some point? Could an earlier human companion have been Chinese? At one stage, concerned that his hip was taking so long to strengthen after the operation—it was months before he'd put his leg down—we took him to a canine naturopath, for massage and acupuncture. He was fine with the person who first treated him, but on the third visit another woman came in—a very nice woman, she seemed, and I've no reason to think otherwise—and Charlie immediately cowered behind our legs, growling, and would not go near her. This woman had tightly curled blond hair and a high-pitched, raspy voice. We've since worked out that that particular combination, for Charlie—the voice, the tight-curled blond hair—is a powerful trigger. Was he once abused by such a person? Who knows? He certainly behaves as if he was.

But enough. Love Charlie as I do, I'm probably not so innocent myself, though the relationship seems to be sufficiently sound for him to treat my blunders with a touch of irony rather than resentment. A dog? Capable of irony? You'd better believe it. (Czesław Miłosz, the great Polish poet: *Irony is the glory of slaves.*[13])

A story.

It was the winter before we moved onto the little farm. T. was down in the city for the day and for reasons I'm about to explain we'd been going to a different park for Charlie's daily walk, but I thought he might be missing his old haunts and

13 A slight misquotation, from his poem "Not This Way": "My voice always lacked fullness, I would like to render a different thanksgiving, / And generously, without irony which is the glory of slaves."

decided to take him back to the "wild" park, so called because on three-and-a-half sides it has a thin border of mountain rainforest, and a few bush tracks. An old, disused road (once a racetrack) runs through it, of maybe two kilometers all up, that you can walk around with your dogs. And at this point in time the local council, in a draconian tightening of the bylaws, was re-designating some parks as "on-leash" that had until then been "off-leash." There was now much less space in which one could walk with one's dog companion off-leash, and the off-leash spaces tended to be the less attractive parks, where dog-fearing humans were less likely to want to go. There were substantial on-the-spot fines for those who did not obey.

The procedure was very controversial. Whole dog communities were being disrupted. Our "wild" park was now strictly an on-leash park. The exuberant, windy afternoons of ball throwing and excited dogs racing about the wide cleared area were suddenly a thing of the past. Council rangers patrolled the old road or even (yes) lurked in the bushes along it, in the hope of catching and fining offenders.

Charlie's not an on-leash dog. Since this new council regime had begun, we'd been taking him to a smaller park in the next town, five kilometers away, crowded with loud and unfriendly dogs he didn't know. I'd decided, this afternoon, to try the wild park anyway, regardless of the risk of a fine. We drove along a dirt track I'd discovered, to a little-used entrance, left the car there, and, starting from this different point, began our customary circuit, across the old road, into the large, cleared area, then onto the bush path on the other side that would eventually lead us back to the old road and, one hundred meters or so along it, the car.

We met no other people or dogs. It seems the council policy was working. But Charlie, oblivious to all that, was loving being back in his old haunt, following his favorite route. We took our time. I had a lead with me—Charlie must have thought it strange I'd carry it here—but it seemed I wasn't going to have to use it. Until, that is, I thought I glimpsed, just as we were rounding a bend, a flash of council-ranger-jacket orange in the bushes ahead. Hopefully we hadn't yet been seen. I called Charlie over, urgently, *sotto voce*, and, to his great puzzlement and annoyance, fastened the leash to his collar.

It was nothing. There was no ranger. My paranoia. Almost back at the car, on a grassy clearing by the racetrack, I unfastened his lead. He turned his back to me and—something he'd never done before and has never done since—raised his hind leg and, ironically, disdainfully, in an exquisite expression of annoyance at my bizarre and inexcusable behavior, peed on my foot.

❦

Have I changed my mind about Charlie's dusk anxiety? I'm not sure I have. Although I've been sounding various reasons for it—loneliness, isolation, grief, some trauma from his earlier life—that trembling still takes place at dusk. Of course there are people—some of them supposedly experts in dog behavior (we're about to meet one of them)—who'd say his trembling is first and foremost attention seeking, and that, if it's increased, it's because we've reinforced it by responding to it. And to tell the truth, if a part of me wants to reject this outright, another isn't so sure, though for reasons a dog psychologist might not accept.

What if, whether he's conscious of it or not, there *were* some sort of attention seeking—some sort of performative component—to Charlie's trembling? Is there something necessarily wrong with that? Mightn't there be a different way of reading such things? I can't put aside the thought that there *is* a kind of communication going on, encouraged (reinforced) by the fact that the trembling *has* been responded to. Whatever else Charlie's trembling has done it's made us *look*, made us *think* about him, made us *wonder*. *Follow me*, it could almost be saying (*Charlie* could almost be saying), *into myself*. Or perhaps, less ambitiously, more in keeping with his probable understanding of the human, *away from yourself*.

All of which must make it sound as if this is going to be a book about Charlie. While I'll admit that that was my initial intention, it's not going to be quite like that. Instead it seems as if he's been sent as psychopomp, to lead me somewhere—*across* something, *to* something—though where and what that thing is I don't think I can yet quite say. Sometimes one can't see for looking.

A Laocoön

November 2012. At the little farm now, with the old white van I've just bought in the long, rutted driveway, its side freshly painted with the number 269[14] and its back open upon one of the last loads from the house in Railway Parade. Tim the handyman, "lent" us by the real estate agents, has already cleaned the upper room of the cabin, sanded and oiled the floor, patched and painted the walls, liberated windows that hadn't been opened in decades, so that, onto old bookshelves I've yet to locate (they're supposedly the van's next task), I can begin to unpack my library—my safety blanket, T. calls it (or so I imagine she does): a thousand books of poetry, a thousand novels, hundreds of works of literary theory, criticism, philosophy, politics, history, art, an embarrassing proportion of which I've never read but which (how to put this?) have always seemed to *anchor* me somehow, in ways it would take a separate volume to explain. We eat our first meals, sleep our first nights (so many *roosters* in this little valley!), meet our

14 The ear tag of a calf found by activists in an Israeli industrial farming facility in May 2012 was 269. In a protest which rapidly, if briefly, sparked an international movement, some of these activists had themselves branded with the number. Others have simply had themselves tattooed with it, or painted it on their vans.

first neighbors, sow our first seeds, make our first mistakes, and before we know it—but two months have passed!—we are five, not three.

For years already we'd been wanting to do more for animals than just donate to charities and attend protests, and from the moment T. discovered it on the real estate site the thought that there might be room for rescued animals had been a large part of this little farm's appeal. But perhaps we should have kept the idea to ourselves a little longer. We moved in in early October. It was scarcely the end of November when a friend alerted us to a card she'd seen on the noticeboard in the food co-op, seeking a home for two already rescued sheep for whom their current carers had insufficient grass.

We went to the co-op, wrote down the details, dialed the number, and two days later were backing into a paddock, van open and ready, another three towns down on the east side of the mountains. There were four sheep there. We could take our pick. "These two," said Don, one of the resident humans, pointing to a large, regal ewe and her slightly smaller friend, "came here with us two years ago, Mary and Billie, but those"—pointing to the ram and wether—"brought themselves here six months ago; we simply don't have enough feed for all of them." It was true: the paddock, between the two rows of towering poplars, had been grazed to the level of a late-summer cricket pitch.

"Brought themselves?"

"Yes," said Sue, Don's partner. "There's a paddock next door, also grazed bare. We don't know who owns it. It's separated from this place by a huge hedge of privet and cotoneaster. No one ever comes. There were two sheep in there. We'd no idea. And I guess when they realized that there were ewes on this side they began to eat their way through. Suddenly, one morning, they were here, and no amount of coaxing would get them to go back. They were huge with wool—never been shorn—but we dealt with that and they've been here a year. Now there's nothing left for them to eat."

But which to take? Mary and the ram had apparently become good friends, so perhaps we should take them, or Billie and the wether, and yet Mary and Billie had grown up together, as very likely had the wether and ram. Mary and Billie "belonged" to the place; the ram and wether were newcomers, if only to that side of the cotoneaster. Clearly it had to be them. Thenceforth, having taken their friends away, we'd find ourselves referring to Mary and Billie as The Lonely Ewes.

We were surprised, when it came time to leave, how easy the ram and wether were to load. A handful of grain was enough to entice them. I remember various things about the trip back. One is how quiet it was. Another is how fascinated Charlie, in the middle of the front seat, was with the creatures behind him. I don't think he and the ram took their eyes off one another the whole journey. At some point T. asked, rhetorically I think, what their names were. I don't remember who said what, but by the time we got back they were Jonathan (the wether) and Henry-Lee: "Henry-Lee" from a Nick Cave song we'd been listening to, and "Jonathan" from Jonathan Swift, though in truth he looks, from one angle, far more like the middle-aged Ezra Pound, goatee and all. Almost immediately, when they stepped out at the little farm, they took possession of the place.

All of which must give the impression that this chapter is about sheep, but we're not quite there. There's one more Charlie incident to incorporate before, his dusk anxiety mysteriously resolving—is it this place?—he steps a little to the side, to take up his role as farm foreman.

Normally we wouldn't have much to do with a dog trainer, but in this case it was she who came to us. We'd only told a handful of friends about our refuge dream, but the needs of animals are great, and word spreads quickly. One evening, *at* dusk, Carol—a stranger, with a strong Polish accent—arrived, talking already as she strode along the veranda, about how sorry she was to interrupt but she was here about a dog who needed rescuing. Could we give him a home?

By this stage we'd had Jonathan and Henry barely a week and were just settling them in. How would *they* react to a second dog? Of even greater concern was the fact that Charlie had been viciously attacked only the day before and was still under observation. Another dog—and a traumatized one at that—seemed too much to take on. But you can't always control the timing or let it dictate your responses. We didn't say no outright. Instead we agreed to meet this dog, Kenny, and to see how he and Charlie got along. It wasn't essential, perhaps, that Charlie like him, but it was certainly desirable.

But that's another story. Kenny didn't come to live with us. We met him three times. On the first two occasions there'd been no negative signs, though few positive ones either. He and Charlie seemed fairly uninterested in one another. But on the third there was an incident. Charlie picked up Kenny's ball, in play, and Kenny went for him. He was shouted off immediately, but, so soon after Charlie had been so badly attacked, it was enough. We said no, and that wasn't the point I was making anyway. The point is about dog training. Twice during the Kenny business Carol noticed Charlie's trembling, and that T. would pick him up and comfort him. That was bad practice, apparently, a dog-training mistake. We were *reinforcing* his trembling. We should instead pay it no attention, though by now it was probably so deeply engrained that only some strict disciplinary regime could stop it.

Training by love, and training by discipline. It's probably just us and opinions will vary, but we've never been interested in conventional dog training, have thought it an intrusion on a dog's own already very limited space, one more imposition of human will upon them. If you need a dog to heel, to sit tight until given the signal, etc., then perhaps you're bringing him/her into too confined and confining a situation in the first place. But it's complicated. Circumstances vary. There's no question that, especially in an inner city, training (couldn't we think of it as "teaching"?) can save a dog's life, as well as serve the convenience of a human companion.

On December 13—a date lodged in my memory—Charlie was attacked in the park (no longer the wild one, alas) to which he is now taken daily for a walk. Off-leash until four, and I can't walk him on-leash anyway, since I've enough difficulty walking myself and would rather not risk having him trip me or pull me over. The park is an oval sports field, hardly ever used for sport, with a cleared area at one end and scrub at the other. And on this day, until we'd walked almost halfway around, we'd had the place to ourselves. At that point, however, a man with two dogs, on leashes, began to cross. A larger brown dog, and a pup with markings much like Charlie's. Charlie saw them and, as is his wont, paused, looked in their direction, then tentatively began to make his way over. We were about forty meters apart, the man and I, and at almost the halfway point Charlie seemed to have decided that these dogs were okay—T. says he must have thought they were friends (he's shortsighted) or he wouldn't have done this—and that he could go right up to them.

But he was mistaken. The moment he came within range the larger, brown dog lunged and got him by the neck. Charlie went from sniffing curiosity to blood-curdling shrieking within a split second. I got there as quickly as I could and by the time I arrived the man—a lean man in his mid-forties, tall, deeply tanned, close-shaven, with a goatee and much-tattooed arms—was punching and punching his dog in the face trying to make him let go. Two people can't pry at the same time at a bull terrier's jaws, and I stood by helpless, albeit relieved a little as it seemed, from what I could see, as if he only had Charlie's ear in his teeth (I was wrong: behind the ear—out of view—he had his teeth locked deep in Charlie's neck).

There was blood everywhere, and the brown dog would not let go (that should be in italics: *would not let go*). I fought the impulse to beat him with my crutch, all I could think of doing,[15] but already I was deeply and traumatically conflicted, terrified for Charlie's distress—that I might be witnessing, powerless, his death—and alarmed that this man should be punching his dog so hard and in the face this way. A gentle afternoon had erupted suddenly into horror.

Eventually—was it five minutes? seven? one?—the brown dog let go. I can't say what made him do so. And Charlie fled. But both the brown dog and the pup had slipped their collars in the wrestling. The brown dog charged and caught Charlie again, twenty meters away, got him by the shoulder and tried to shake him. This time his hold wasn't so fast, however, and Charlie slipped from it almost as soon as the man caught up with them. Charlie fled again—the pup now with him, as if just as anxious to get away from it all—but before I made off after them I asked the man about his hand, which I realized was one of the sources of the blood that now seemed everywhere—all over my stick, my shoes, this man's clothes, the grass. One or another of the dogs had bitten him, either his own as he punched him, or Charlie in his near-mortal distress. I told him he should get the wound attended to, asked him whether he had far to go. He said, very quickly—all this in a blur—that he was staying with his daughter nearby, on Mars Avenue, and that these were her dogs. He said the brown dog hated other dogs, but loved people. That, and that this was the first time he'd ever walked these dogs, and that he was

15 I've been told since that the thing to do is to insert one's finger in the attacking dog's anus.

never going to walk them again.

I was looking down at the brown dog as he said it: he was staring up at me with soft, gentle eyes, as if expecting praise. I'm sure I could have patted him with complete impunity. But I was already scouring the park for Charlie. As I crossed the grass in the direction he'd gone I saw him at the top, heading toward home, the pup with him. By the time I got to the car, however, he'd doubled back, and burst out from the scrub on the other side of the track, leapt into the back seat as soon as I opened the door. The pup was nowhere in sight. I was about to get in and drive off—desperate to get Charlie to the vet—when the youth from the produce store over the main road appeared with the pup in his arms, asking if he was mine. "No," I said, "it's his," gesturing to the man still kneeling with the brown dog in the center of the oval, then said I'd take it over. Charlie, miraculously, seemed as if he was not severely injured. Maybe I had another minute or two to try to get some more details. The man's name, perhaps, or the exact address of his daughter. But by now he'd had time to think of possible consequences and had locked up, as people do. Before I'd even opened my mouth he said, "Don't expect me to tell you anything else; I won't pay any vet bills." I shrugged, told him, again, to look after his hand, get a tetanus shot, then drove off.

The point? Of setting this down? It's threefold. Firstly, it's a major event in Charlie's recent life, and not a minor one in mine, and I'm trying to write about his life—his life amongst others—which is perforce about our lives together. Secondly it's that I wished, then, and for days afterward, that this man, or his daughter, had had that dangerous dog *trained*, so he'd have let go upon command, or never lunged at all. Despite— alongside—all my reservations about training. But it seems he was conditioned in another way. (I'm trying not to say anything about investing dogs with our own personalities.)

And thirdly—more existentially—it's about helplessness, Charlie's and mine, in this incident and out of it.

Of course, our helplessness in one sense—his pinned to the ground, gripped in the powerful jaw of a member of his own species who was trying to kill him, and mine, unable to run to him, unable to use my right hand to try to wrench the other dog away—were of very different kinds, but in another sense perhaps not. I've become used to falling, finding myself suddenly and ignominiously in contact with the floor, the dirt, the asphalt, the pavement, struggling to get to my feet. Briefly but repeatedly like a character from a Beckett novel (*How It Is*). Knowing the *ground* again, cast down, groveling in and before the elements. Abject, as it does seem to me when in the midst of it. Also, perhaps—making the most of it!—the beneficiary of a dark gift. Knowing that one's towering humanness, that supposedly *sets us aside* from other animals, is so fragile; that there is a place, just there (just *here*), a split second away, where all the power of words, of thought—the human edifice— won't help and means nothing, and the vast, ubiquitous crust of civilization seems as thin as a piece of tissue paper.

In this light I see that horrid triptych in the park as something as deeply symbolic as it was deeply real: creatures locked together, a man, two dogs, one of them in the jaws of the other, the man holding the brown dog in a headlock, punching him furiously, the brown dog with his teeth in the neck of the smaller dog, the blood of the man and the dogs intermingling. I keep thinking of the *Laocoön*, that famous sculpture of the man and his two sons being strangled by serpents. Creatures locked in tragedy. Bound fast together in some eternal, wordless relation. Wordless *agony*, I almost wrote, though I'm not sure I'd yet go that far. *Agon*, let me say instead, a painful and perpetual struggle ... when it all might be so different.

A Laocoön

between the two rows of towering poplars

(Billie, Henry, Jonathan, Mary)

The Art of Fencing

Since Jonathan and Henry-Lee arrived it's been a matter of feed and fences. Do *we* have enough grass? Is *our* small field going to be adequate? What other spaces can we find? There are three spaces now, and all have had to be fenced, one part of the place partitioned from another, so that certain plants, bushes, trees, gardens don't get eaten. A process of learning to make temporary fences secure enough so that the sheep won't get through them (Henry, ram that he is, will barge his way; Jonathan is more devious, a Houdini), of testing and repairing the perimeter fences, of fencing some things and creatures *in*, other things and creatures *out*, dealing with—thinking through—unanticipated questions of space.

The sheep have come to us for refuge. Whether they know this or not. Whether they *want* this or not. And our first concern has to be that they're safe. There are large dogs roaming in the area, at least three pairs of them that we've seen so far. One pair, we are told by a neighbor, "belongs" to a dairy farmer a kilometer down the road: they are fine with "stock," our neighbor says, but dangerous to other dogs. The other pairs we just don't know about. Packs of wild dogs are renowned for killing sheep. And there are foxes, feral cats. We must think, too, of the other creatures in this refuge:

the ducks, the rabbits. Our neighbor, Geoff, has a habit of letting his ewes graze on the grassy verge outside our south-side fence—or rather, he realizes that they get out of his own paddock but will sometimes take all day to come and get them. The presence of ewes scarcely a hoof's length away drives Henry crazy: he runs back and forth along that part of the fence, pushes at it, butts it, gets up on his hind legs as if he'd climb over it, testing the old posts to the maximum. His sexual longing is almost palpable, as is the way he torments Jonathan, his only real sexual option.

Do we have a right to keep Henry from the ewes? But of course we have to, and the refuge, on such days, seems almost a prison. It's hard not to worry about his quality of life. Should we seek a ewe to live with us? Would that be fair to her? And could we deal with lambs? A part of "rescue" is liberation from the wheel of exploitative breeding, reproductive slavery, but it isn't as if sheep don't have their own desires, want their own families. Yet if we allow animals in refuges to have the children they no doubt desire, their offspring will take up space badly needed by other abused animals. Suddenly we seem up to our knees in ethical dilemmas. Let Henry out and he may impregnate one of Geoff's ewes, and that lamb will be slaughtered or sold on for breeding purposes. *Don't* let him out and those ewes will become pregnant anyway, to one of *his* rams.

Ethical dilemmas, that's to say, and metaphors, for it's hard, once one's mind has let in the possibility, not to see this matter of fences as metaphor also. Fences in the mind. Fences in language.

T. sits on the veranda, when it's warm enough, researching her thesis, reading about neuroscience, sentience, animal brains, ethology, neural substrates, looking for the words and phrases and concepts that can help press her thinking further, and at the same time always and continuously trying to work out which ones—words, phrases, ideas, concepts—

are *preventing* us from thinking further. Maintaining fences, shifting them, dismantling them, dealing with matters of *in* and *out*. She reads about sheep: what they are supposed to be capable and incapable of, what they are supposed to *be*. And she watches Henry and Jonathan (*don't* give them names, says the traditional wisdom, because then you won't be able to *use* them, by which is meant *kill* them, or to do so readily the other things you "need" to do *to* them—castrate them, dock their tails, cut their horns, cut the skin from around their anus—to have them produce what it is you wish them to produce; but there, we *have* given them names, language is *involved*, in part because we have no intention of killing them or using their wool: another fence set up, or is it broken down?); she *sees* them, Henry and Jonathan, doing things that the books say they do not or cannot do. Charlie and Henry and Jonathan learning from one another. Dog learning from sheep; sheep learning from dog. Charlie, for example, licks Henry's face, as he will do with other, larger dogs. (Carol would probably say it's a "dominance" thing, but what *other* word is "dominance" holding at bay?) And very soon Henry is following Charlie around, licking the air, trying to *tell* Charlie (who understands very well but isn't always in the mood) that he, Henry, *wants to be licked*. Charlie, we joke, thinks he's a sheep, and Henry thinks he's a dog. But no. There is a species barrier (barrier, fence), and they are working at it. And she sits, T., reading, thinking, working at that barrier, too, while I, *avoiding writing* (for it does seem, sometimes, a threatening place, a hard *terrain*), tighten mesh, bolt posts onto posts to increase the height of fences, learn mysteries and secrets and tricks of wire and star pickets, wood and post-hole drills and rapid-set concrete; or she moves a temporary fence, re-thinks a barrier, *avoiding reading*, while I write, or try to. Knowing that a sentence, too, is a fence, that a paragraph is a fence, an essay is a fence, an argument is a fence, and that the arts of making them (clear, tight), and *un*-making them, are also the arts of fencing.[16]

❧

When we first moved into this house, as we were going back and forth collecting loads of papers, books, furniture, clothes, tools, kitchenware from the house on Railway Parade, T. noticed a sheep tethered to a post a few houses up, on a rope that allowed that sheep to come dangerously close to the road. She thought this was carelessness, if not actual abuse of some kind. It was all I could do to persuade her that we shouldn't "rescue" that sheep, that we weren't yet ready to turn the new house into a refuge. The next day, in any case, the sheep was

16 Of course, one of the most insidious fences in a book like this is the narrative itself. To be open to animals it's possible we'll need different kinds of narrative. As it stands, a "normative" narrative tends to hide or sequester animals, denying them much access to and influence upon the author's wider world. An early reader of this manuscript expressed disappointment that it wasn't, as they'd expected, a book about my and T.'s life together here in the mountains—or rather that it was only inconsistently so. It had gaps, shifts of style and register. Fair enough, but we are not, T. and I, the focus. Such a narrative as there is here is perhaps better thought of as *a narrative turned upside down*: the animals that are normally suppressed or swallowed by a story, or serve as accessory to it, have been brought toward the fore, and the "humans" play more of a supporting role. And almost certainly— particularly from the (imagined) perspective of animals themselves— this process won't go far enough. On the one hand one has to negotiate with readers' expectations—too much strangeness and one defeats one's purpose—and, on the other, *getting over oneself* is a complicated process. (Such diffidence, in entering "the space of the Animal"! Such presumption and awkwardness. Yet we, too, are animals. Humankind has worked for thousands of years to build this barrier between itself and other creatures, to suppress and occlude and discount the animal within ourselves—that *is* ourselves—and now there is this immense work of undoing.)

gone. And although I did, later, see her for myself, tethered to the fence of an abandoned house a little further along, it was only the once: clearly she'd been moved elsewhere. Later, we began to see a family walking a sheep on a lead along the road outside. Neither of us realized that it was the same sheep. And so it was we had a visitor—or rather visitors—a few weeks after Charlie's attack.

Later, that's to say—three months after we moved in, and just a few weeks after our own sheep had arrived—we saw this family, a mother, father, and two young girls, walking by with their sheep, and T., engaging them in conversation at the gate, eventually invited them in to meet Jonathan and Henry-Lee. But what was at first a friendly encounter became difficult. Ethics again. Dilemma again. Their sheep is a ewe. And she'd recently given birth. We asked about the lamb, and they said, a little awkwardly, that it wasn't with them. They explained that the ewe was a beloved pet, but that they also wanted her for her milk, and that it was, after all, a kind of contract: she was living with them, and since they were feeding her and giving her shelter, it was only reasonable that she give them milk, a simple exchange. They were thinking of "introducing" her to a ram again next year, to repeat the process. It was evident that they'd planned her pregnancy—this first lamb—all along. The pregnancy, and the removal of the lamb. On my part (*was it too far-fetched?*) I couldn't help but think of the story of Abraham and Isaac. God's asking Abraham to sacrifice Isaac; Abraham's building the fire, whetting the knife.

We are not gods. And even if it were permissible to enter a one-sided "contractual" arrangement with a creature who has no understanding of contracts—at least not in *this* way, for it seems clear enough to me that animals (the sheep and the dog, anyway) have a fair sense of justice; and love, trust, are, after all, *contractual*—could it ever extend to asking a ewe to (a) accept what might in effect be rape, and (b) sacrifice her child? But of course there was—is—no asking. And no "contract." And no choice in the matter. *Animals do not owe us rent.* To the ewe it can seem only that her child is stolen. That these human creatures who feed, pet, and walk her also take her children away.

Do you see what I am doing? (Have *I*, before this, seen what I am doing?) I am following the sheep into something. What is it, this something? Ah, but how could it (yet) have a *name*? Do you believe me, that there *is* something? Derrida, in *The Animal That Therefore I Am*, writes about the embarrassment of standing naked before his cat. How the gaze of the animal humiliates philosophy (he doesn't actually say "humiliates," but that's clearly what it is; he also, elsewhere, talks about philosophy *trembling*). I think I am writing about that, though I would hope that it's not only that.

And Charlie? It must seem as if I've abandoned him, there at the vet's, after he'd been savaged by one of his own. But no, he's fine. Four months later even the fur had grown back where he'd been so cruelly exposed by the razer. The vet, Mark, explained the danger of puncture wounds from another dog's teeth: how the teeth, as they penetrate, drive bacteria deep into the flesh, so that stubborn infections, abscesses, are a real concern. He gave us antibiotics, antiseptic cream, painkillers, and told us to come back in the morning, having ensured that Charlie hadn't eaten, so he could give him a general anesthetic to enable him to clean the wound carefully and stitch it closed. He also explained how, when a powerful dog shakes another in his or her jaws—a killing motion—the victim's skin can be torn loose from the flesh beneath, severing innumerable small blood vessels, causing extensive bruising and eventually, possibly, a dangerous necrosis of the skin. By the morning, he said, the bruising, if this had happened, should have become readily apparent.

When we collected Charlie the next afternoon he was

groggy, his neck and his shoulder shaved bare, the wound beneath the stitches still seeping, but the report was good. There was no extensive bruising. The chance of necrosis was slim. If we kept up the antibiotics the puncture wound should also be okay. After a few days both Charlie and I were getting over our trauma—Charlie, in T.'s opinion, more quickly than I. (But how can we know? there can be psychological and emotional bruising, too, and perhaps, of a kind, necrosis …)

But it wasn't over. A week after the attack T., arriving with Charlie at the park, saw a man there with two dogs, a larger brown one and a pup with markings like Charlie's. Neither was on a leash. They didn't speak, she and the man. She didn't approach him, and he, as soon as he saw our car, leashed the dogs and walked off.

We saw him again, one or the other of us, three or four times in the month following. So much for never taking them to the park again. Mark had urged us to report the incident, and although I was reluctant at first—the man, after all, had suffered some injury trying to make his dog release Charlie, and had said he wouldn't ever walk the dogs again—these repeated sightings led me to think I should do what I could to ensure at the least that the brown dog was muzzled when taken out in public. More than that I didn't want. I couldn't see that the dog should be punished for the stupidity and carelessness—projected aggression—of his "owner" (another word, another fence). But my first report was too diffident. A ranger from the council was supposed to contact me, but nothing happened. Then Elizabeth, an elderly friend who walks her old and nearly blind dog in the same park, told T. one day that she'd been approached by an aggressive man with a brown dog and a smaller, younger dog with markings like Charlie's, and told by him that she'd better make sure her dog didn't go anywhere near his, or his dog would "tear it apart." There was another, younger man at the park at the time, with two dogs of his own, but this aggressive man had not approached him. Elizabeth felt he'd chosen her to abuse because she was elderly and vulnerable. She was shaken; she talked about never taking her dog to the park again.

This time at the council—I had come with Elizabeth, at her request—I lodged a more formal complaint. A ranger came to see me later the same day to verify my statement, and Charlie greeted her, barking at the gate. She saw immediately the shaved patches and the extent of the attack. If she could locate the offending dog and "owner," and that owner did not agree to muzzle the dog whenever it was taken off the property, she had the option of imposing a fine and, that failing to bring about any change, of having the dog declared dangerous. That, however, might mean the death of the dog, she said, as having a dog declared dangerous entailed a considerable expense in the installation of cages and fences, let alone the constraints imposed upon taking the dog out in public. Many owners chose instead to shoot their dogs or have them "put down."

As I feared, the act of reporting the incident meant it had slipped into language, system, narrative. It had been *taken away from itself*; a label had been given, and the victim, very likely the only victim, would be the non-human animal, the already victim. Even if the owner were to comply with a dangerous dog order, what kind of life would it be for the dog, perpetually caged, muzzled anytime it was taken out in public? Again an ethical dilemma, if it hadn't gone past that already.[17] Sometimes it can feel as if one is standing at a fence, convinced that the ethical solution is on the other side, if only one can find one's way through. But perhaps ethics,

---

17   And I think it might have. A few months later, as I was walking Charlie at the edge of the park, a man in a white car drove by, slowed down opposite me, shouted through his open window that I had ruined his life, threatened to kill me if he ever saw me again. What story there?

too, are themselves a kind of fence. In helping the human world manage itself, they also help it gel, hold together against whatever it rubs against.

Meanwhile there were real fences to attend to, and the matter of grass. Could the little farm support two sheep? The rule of thumb, apparently, is one sheep per acre. Should we replace the rickety middle fence? Get a gate put in it so the sheep could graze the lush grass on the other side of the swamp? Repair the causeway of old railway sleepers across the swamp, so that the sheep could get to the grass in the first place? And before that, wouldn't we need to build a fence down there across the north side of the property, where at the moment it's open to the poorly fenced bush block next door? A fence over a swamp. How to do that?

The Grass Library

Winters are cold here in the mountains, if only by comparison with the city below. Every thousand meters above sea level, they say, the temperature drops seven degrees Celsius, and we're just over a thousand meters up. One chilly morning, not long after we moved in, needing a length of wire, I went down to the old galvanized iron shed tacked on to the eastern end of the cabin, and stood in the open side of it, looking about me. I felt the warmth of the northern sun on my back and realized that, for all the debris the previous owners had left here, all the generations of chickens and rats that had lived out their lives nesting amongst it, for all the rusted star pickets, bails of wire, bits of old chain, boxes, jars, tins and plastic containers of nails and bolts and screws (one of them, rusted shut, a tin for Dr. Pat's Irish Mixture, the pipe tobacco my father used), cans of long-separated and solidified paint, containers of old engine oil, parts of long-gone lawn mowers, rusted rakes, broken shovels and hoes, here, *in potential*, at the top of the rise, looking out on forest and swamp gully and the hidden valley, warmed by the eastern and lit by the northern sun, could be a writing room, clean, if I worked hard at the cleaning, uncluttered, if I threw enough away, well lighted, if I could find the right windows and put them in the right places. All I needed—and this part, I admit, seemed insurmountable—was a builder who understood and was prepared to undertake the job. But I found one (bless her), and, ten months later, six after she finished it (for it had taken a long time, unburdening, straightening the farm around it, breaking free, to prepare myself to enter), it was there—is here—quietly waiting, receiving the sound of cicadas, of wind in the peppermint gums and stringybarks and mountain ash trees, of birds, of sheep in the half-paddock just below. A room lined and ceilinged with Gyprock and floored with recycled red cedar, the north and half the eastern side windowed from old mountain houses, a tall, thin window on the southern side where, as I write, a butterfly—a rich, dark brown creature with, on its wings, broad orange chevrons that are like riverbeds of golden sand in a landscape of dark alluvial soil seen from the air—is sitting motionless (a "sword-grass brown," I find it's called); a room painted white to catch and amplify the light, with extensive bookshelves to hold my lifelong companions, whether or not I have or will ever read them, a sturdy, capacious desk ($60 from a man in Richmond), a reading chair, a small sofa, a low sofa-high table (given to us by Judy, a neighbor in Darghan Street, just before she died), for whenever I need to spread papers. A room I hardly dare enter unless my mind and mood are right, since there seems, suddenly, to be such challenge, such responsibility here. Though for what is hard to say (this book?). The saying is part of the challenge.

❧

Once, in my late teens, I was invited to a party on the outskirts of Canberra at a property a fellow student was looking after while the owner was away. I've no idea who the owner was. He or she remains a mystery to this day. It was a big, old house—

old, anyway, in Australian terms—perhaps dating from the mid–nineteenth century, with verandas on all sides, a bull-nosed galvanized iron roof, large, poorly lit rooms with musty sofas, cushions, peeling wallpaper. We drank wine, smoked marijuana, lit a fire for atmosphere although the evening was mild, played guitar, played records, talked. I don't recall it as a crowded affair. Nor can I remember who invited me. Out in the dark—I'd glimpsed them before sunset—were several acres of grazing land, though whether or not they were part of this property I don't know (I've always imagined they were). The nearest neighbor might have been two hundred meters away. There were large, old trees near the house, figs, oaks, casuarinas, paperbarks (we weren't far from the Molonglo River). And at one point, perhaps bored by the conversation inside, or seeing that I was, the host took me out to show me the shed. I don't know why. Perhaps they knew I was studying literature. Perhaps I'd been boring them with my talk about it.

It was a woolshed, not that I know much about woolsheds. I went to a Bachelors and Spinsters Ball in a woolshed once, far out in the west of New South Wales, on the night after a bushfire had gone by (I'd spent that night "fighting" it), and I've slept in one, without the owner's knowing, while hitchhiking to a rock festival (I remember lying there, in my sleeping bag, on the floor of hardwood slabs made almost shiny by the lanolin from the thousands of sheep who'd been shorn there), but I don't know whether these things happened before or after this particular party.

Coated with galvanized iron, *this* shed, which my friend-of-a-friend called the Library, had been lined—Gyprocked—and given a new floor (beneath which I can imagine the old, lanolined floor still sleeping). There were bookcases almost all the way around the walls, a large, angled display table near the door, and at least one row of squat, thigh-high bookcases down the center, and to my further surprise (it was late summer) it was air-conditioned. I remember feeling slightly chilled, though this might have been awe.

I don't think my host was showing it to me alone. I seem to remember other people in the room, two or three. But I was left almost immediately to wander about by myself. I remember that on the display table—centered, as if the pride of the vast collection—was a copy of Sir Walter Raleigh's *A Historie of the World*, opened to its frontispiece and title page. I don't remember which edition it was, but my hunch, given what else I found in that Library, was that it was the first, of 1614. For I also found a copy of what must have been the second folio of Shakespeare, of 1632, and first editions of Defoe's *Robinson Crusoe*, Burton's *Anatomy of Melancholy*, Swift's *Gulliver's Travels*, Pope's *Dunciad*. Indeed it seemed I had only to think of some rare book from my at that point very limited knowledge of literary history (I was just beginning my second year of English) and I'd find it. Dryden's translation of the *Aeneid*, Butler's *Hudibras*, Spratt's magical and bizarre *History of the Royal Society* with accompanying volumes of the *Philosophical Transactions*.[18] And, elsewhere in the room, in the Modern section, first editions of *The Waste Land*, of Yeats, of Oscar Wilde, of Ezra Pound.

How long was I there? An hour? Two? And what did I do afterward? I can't remember. The effect upon me was profound, yet I've hardly ever spoken about it in the decades

18 No doubt, as were most of the other volumes just mentioned, bound in calfskin. Although I don't think I would mention it to the boys, I can't let a reference to the *Philosophical Transactions* pass without noting the account to be found therein (number 30, 9 December 1667) of a transfusion, on November 23 of that year, of sheep blood into the veins of a Mr. Arthur Coga. The long-term effects of this transfusion are not known—did he die of blood poisoning? did he dream of green meadows? did he turn into a sheep?—though it is recorded that Mr. Coga felt so well in the short term that he requested (and was eventually given) a second transfusion.

since. It's as if, even as it was happening, I was taking the experience into me, to a place so deep it could only be retrieved when *it* deemed it was right to do so, when it could be sure that nothing could damage it. A paradox, of course, for whoever "owned" these works—an antiquarian book dealer? a retired professor of English?—seemed to have been so foolish or so trusting as to leave them in the hands of my acquaintance, so that I could hold them in my own, yes, but with no guarantee at all that one or another of them might not have been stolen—perhaps a whole truckload!—by someone less in awe or less scrupulous.

The entire experience, now that it rises again, seems so unlikely that it might have been a dream. But, if it was (it wasn't), it's a dream I've carried about with me for decades. The riches of literature, brought to a galvanized-iron shed, on the edge of Australian paddocks—the ghosts of sheep wandering through it, living sheep grazing about it—as if to a resting place, or there were some accounting, some reconciliation to be done there, some validation (or rejection), through the scrutiny of grass.

❧

My writing room was never a woolshed. It's the old farm shed, no more, though that *was* made of galvanized iron, which I've never removed, and—the mystery of its horseshoes solved—I've learnt it once stabled a racehorse (another ghost about the place). Sheep graze around it nevertheless, and, while I am here (and sometimes when I'm not), enter at will. From my desk I look out upon the close-grazed grass, the tall peppermint and ash and stringybark trees, and on the swamp below. My mind is filled with what I see, and it sometimes feels as though whatever I am thinking or writing has somehow to wander through and make its terms with it (the sheep, the grass, the trees, the swamp ...) before it can settle upon the page. In the top room of the cabin—the room I've come to call the Library—are at least three thousand books (just today I have gone to it for Rilke's *Poems* and Burton's *Anatomy*), and down here, in the writing room, a thousand more.

I should dust them more often.

Undoings

A young Japanese man came to see me recently to talk about writing. His spoken English wasn't great—he'd been in Australia to improve it—but he was well read in contemporary literature in other languages through translation. He was a fan, for example, of W.G. Sebald, author of *The Rings of Saturn*, *Austerlitz*, *Campo Santo*, and other remarkable works, who died tragically in 2001.[19] When this came up I spoke about the challenge Sebald presents, for me but maybe for Australian writers more generally. Sebald's perambulations[20]—his narrator is always traveling, almost always walking (the Suffolk coast, the roads of Corsica …)—draw deeply upon the rich human history of the places he moves through. You might love Sebald's

19 In a car accident, at fifty-seven. "By degrees the bracken thinned," he writes in a memorable passage of which, for copyright reasons, I should quote no further and say no more other than that it involves the author, who has come upon a herd of swine, stepping over a fence and approaching one of them, touching its back and stroking it behind one ear until at length it sighs "like one enduring endless suffering," *The Rings of Saturn*, 1995, trans. Michael Hulse (1998 rpt; Vintage, 2002), 66.

20 I'd rather call them *peripatations*, after the peripatetic (walking) philosophers, but find, alas, that the word doesn't exist (I've been using it for decades).

style and want to adapt it to Australian circumstances, but here you have only two hundred years of settler history, and the indigenous history before that is essentially out of reach, culturally and ethically, for most non-indigenous writers.

If Sebald, wherever he goes, can draw upon a fullness, the non-indigenous Australian who would adapt him has to make a kind of fullness out of what must seem, within Western parameters, more like emptiness. This apparent emptiness, I was saying, is at once our difference, as an invader literature, and our challenge—though for so long so many have seen it as a burden. It stimulates us to turn outward, away from the human (say), and to fill our minds and pages with things we might not hitherto have seen as capable of filling them, let alone as a desirable means of so doing. We must reconfigure this apparent emptiness as a fullness—which is to say *discover* its fullness. We must *open*, *turn away*, at least to some extent, from what until now we've thought constituted and explained us. And this isn't just an aesthetic challenge. If that were all it was I don't think I'd be much interested, nor do I think that those who might see it principally as such would really be able to do it.

The point, and irony, is that it's also a necessity, in our time and for the planet. History, fascinating as it might be (especially to those who don't "have" it), is also a fearsome thing, with a powerful grip—a bewilderment of fences, if you like—and there's a sense in which to be free from it can be a liberation, a gift, though the process of acquiring and realizing and employing that gift will entail, perhaps for a long time yet, strangeness, loneliness, apparent isolation, dislocation, self-doubt, resistance, to say nothing of a likely absence of an audience that understands, appreciates, applauds, and rewards what you are doing—things upon which artists, in their generic isolation, tend so much to depend.

For me, I was thinking this morning, this situation is developing another dimension. Although I won't dispute that I might go back to it, there's a large part of me that, at least for the time being, doesn't much want to write about the *human* anymore, not in the way the contemporary writer might be expected to do. Writers around me—the more "engaged" ones, anyway—are concerned with human rights, resistance to oppression, sexual freedoms, politics, economics, social structures, etc., or are concerned with the human more intimately, in their preoccupation with human feelings, human predicaments, human relationships, love, pain, depression, loneliness (rescue, revelation); or with history, with travel (etc., etc.: perhaps I don't need to go on). But, *having gone to the side of the animal* (awkward and suspect as such a formulation is; let me say rather gone to the fence, to look *through* it), there's a sense in which these things, many of them, have come to seem secondary and even selfish, the day-to-day life and culture of an oppressor, much of the effect if not purpose of which is to blind or distract them (the oppressors) from the fact of that oppression, and therefore to sustain it, to enable it to continue.

Books, for example, have been my life for so long: my guides, my best friends, my saviors even. But we seem to have reached a crossroads. The joy of a new novel has changed, at first into a kind of anxious apprehension, and eventually into clear and simple disinclination, from having experienced too often, as a vegan, the dismay and frustration of characters for whom one is in other ways strongly encouraged to feel affinity and concern, eating roast lamb, fish, steak tartare, etc., or hunting, or fishing, or engaging in some other form of animal abuse or instrumentalization, with apparently no ethical compunction whatsoever on their own or their writer's part.

A friend—not my Japanese visitor, but a vegan who is also a refugee advocate and champion of human rights—recently presented me with another and far darker example. We were talking of asylum seekers, and our disgust at the way they've been treated by a succession of Australian governments. The conversation drifted to boat people and recent tragedies on the Timor Sea and off the coast of Lampedusa, and to footage we'd seen of desperate rescue attempts, the arrival of survivors, their being issued meals and clothes to wear. I couldn't help but wonder what food they'd been given. Ham sandwiches, we supposed. "It is so sad," my friend (whom I may have invented) said suddenly, "to think that with every life you save, unless that person's a vegan, you're condemning an incalculable number of animals to death. If only, in saving a life, you could somehow guarantee that that person you saved wouldn't eat meat anymore"—but of course this thought, to the un-converted, is absurd, ridiculous, even totalitarian. A dilemma. A paradox. A chasm. I can't imagine either of us not saving a human *or* non-human life if it were at all within our power to do so, let alone advocating such a guarantee, but my friend's reflection seems so perfect an example of the dark places that can open up when one tries to meld or reconcile two very different *ethoi*, the way such attempts can lead one into strange and confronting territory, where human rights and animal rights seem irreconcilable, and either choice one makes, if one *can* make a choice, will seem a crime.[21]

---

21 Not all of these dark places are so speculative. Note the Australian government's adoption of U.S.-style "ag-gag" laws, which in effect make it a (human) crime to expose the fact that other humans are perpetrating (human) crimes against animals. One is not, by law, allowed to mistreat animals, even in the process of slaughtering them, but not only has the Australian government (like so many others) made it a crime to film such abuse in order to expose it, it also fails to supply sufficient people to adequately inspect slaughterhouses and intensive farming institutions for such violations, and insists that such violations, when found (when? how? by whom?) be reported to an organization so compromised by its relations to the meat industry that the government can be confident its responses to any crimes reported will not rock the boat.

I've written of *having gone to the side of the animal*, but of course that in itself is a kind of dream. (It's not even, as T. reminds me, the right way to say it: humans are animals, too; we're speaking here of having gone to the side of the *non-human* animal.) On the one hand you just can't *leave* the human: all you can do is create a kind of unsettlement between yourself and a great deal of your immediate environment— exile yourself, as it were, in large part by making yourself a source of unsettlement to others, whether you seek to do this or not—and on the other hand the *non*-human animal can't and won't let you in. Indeed it might even be that you don't want it to; that to "let you in" would not in any way be good for that non-human animal. You are stuck in the middle, neither.

"There is something *existential* about this then?" asked my Japanese friend. And yes, bingo: existential. Yet also not. Existential in that sense of living in the moment, or at least trying to, amongst what is most immediately around you, and in the rejection of the force of history, and also I think in Existentialism's insistence on taking responsibility (or at least trying to) for one's own actions and decisions. If only there were not also Existentialism's relentless insistence upon the human. But then that's the way it's been, with philosophy, always. And why the gaze of the animal (*cum* Derrida's cat, whose gaze, in the bathroom, makes Derrida so uncomfortable) leaves the philosopher naked.[22]

✺

Sometimes, as one writes—*following* the writing, letting it *lead*—one can find oneself suddenly in a strange and sacred

22 A situation I've written about elsewhere. See "The Loaded Cat" in *Derrida's Breakfast* (Brandl & Schlesinger, 2016).

place. As if, walking through an unfamiliar terrain, exploring it, lost in it, one broke into a clearing, amongst tall, majestic trees, with strange stones there, the remnants of an ancient temple, a sacred site.[23] So, today, thinking again of Charlie's dusk anxiety, "trembling" has led me to a memory of Derrida, who has said that there are things before which philosophy trembles—things, like "the Question of the Animal," which shake it to its core—and, beyond him, to a distant recollection of reading Kierkegaard, as once, long ago, I tried to do, and thence to *Fear and Trembling*, that strange work of his "John of the Silence" (Kierkegaard used many pseudonyms) and the story of Abraham (which Kierkegaard discusses there), which, since we focus so much upon Isaac, we forget is also a story of a *non*-human animal, a sheep, caught in a thorn bush (what is that? the thicket of human thinking?), taking the weight of Abraham's trembling.

Dare I go back to Charlie here, *his* trembling (as a *plea*? an anxious *invitation*?)?

⚜

What are we really doing when we "rescue" a sheep, a pig, a chicken, a calf, from the certain slaughter they would eventually suffer in the industrial process, to say nothing of the suffering they'd experience en route? There is about it a distressing and unsettling randomness. "Rescuing" one, two, a dozen, even a hundred animals, can never halt and perhaps in some way even obliquely supports the slaughter we try to save them from. Another dilemma. For if we *don't* do it, *don't* rescue, we sanction, we give permission *to* that process, and perhaps also serve—by removing opposition from sight, by condoning such removal—to support the effacement, the removal from mind,

---

23 Sacred? Perhaps toxic would be a better term here.

that is the process's greatest strategy and ally.

There is also a question of hierarchy. Most people, when the word "refuge" is used, think at first of a *wildlife* refuge. There are people who've been surprised that we'd begin by giving refuge to sheep rather than, say, injured kangaroos, although in truth there is no *rather* in this: it's simply that the sheep have come or been brought to us, and kangaroos haven't (though wild ducks have, possums have, snakes have, and there are swamp wallabies about). And the field that the sheep now occupy has rabbits in it. Rabbits are seen as a problem in Australia, at times and in many areas a "pest," even a "plague" (just as, ironically, kangaroos have been held to be). Many would consider it's one's responsibility to kill them. And there are rats in the compost, and in the old chicken coop which the sheep now use for shelter, and probably in the walls of the house (there are many rats in the town nearby—a side it downplays—and so of course there are refugees); it's one's responsibility, in the eyes of many, to kill these also. There is a cat, too, who visits from a neighbor's house, and cats kill native birds. Then there is the matter of the birds themselves. There are many native birds here—wattlebirds, bowers, blue wrens, finches, currawongs, white cockatoos, black cockatoos, crimson lorikeets, plovers, butcherbirds, peewits, and more— but there are also Indian mynahs, which are *non*-native and seen as a pest, driving out native birds from their habitat. I have mynahs in the roof of my cabin. What am I to do? Kill them, too? Block off their entrances, thereby perhaps walling in fledglings, separating parents from children, condemning one or the other to death?

There are so many old, rusty binaries involved here. The matter of clean versus unclean, for example. Human wisdom has it that certain creatures—rats, mice, cockroaches, etc.— are unclean, and encourages their elimination. But whose is the uncleanliness? Are humans asking animals to take the rap for their own, human uncleanliness? (Ah, but a cockroach is an *insect*, not an *animal*: another issue and another hierarchy.) In most instances these creatures encroach on human spaces because material in those spaces attracts and sustains them. Keep an unclean kitchen, for example, and you invite them. (Might it also have something to do with *what* we eat? A cockroach can smell a tiny skerrick of meat from a great distance.) Shift the perspective. Maybe these creatures are not so much unclean in themselves, as cleaning up after *us*.

We categorize animals, and behave toward them—accord or refuse them protection or sanctuary—depending upon whether we see them as *wild* or *tame, feral* or *domesticated, native* or *exotic, rare* or *common, endangered* or *of least concern, pet* or *pest, livestock* or otherwise. In most instances, classification on one side of one of these binaries will lead us to "value" an animal more than classification on the other. In most instances, too, such classification masquerades as recognition of some value inherent in the animal itself. Yet of course in all instances these classifications reflect *human* culture, *human* self-interest, *human* value. Hierarchies are matters of perspective and power. Arguably they're so important to us because we are so keen to see ourselves on the upside of them.

An example recently to hand is the bilby, a long-eared desert-dwelling Australian marsupial currently on the list of endangered species. A bilby conservation area has been set up in far western Queensland, surrounded by fences intended to keep out predators. Flooding recently damaged these fences. Before conservationists could assess the damage, some one hundred and fifty offspring of these rare creatures (creatures, it should be said—a perennial Australian circumstance— whose numbers have declined largely because of human incursion upon and damage to bilby habitat) had been killed by feral cats. Within two weeks of the damage being realized, according to the news report, some 3,000 cats had been shot in the area. And here, again, is an ethical dilemma. Clearly the life of a feral cat—an exotic pet that has become wild—is seen as worth far less than that of an endangered bilby. But why is this so? The logic here seems to be the same logic that makes a 1930 Australian penny, of which there were only a handful produced, worth far, far more than a 1960 penny, of which millions were produced. The logic of the coin collector, or of the stamp collector (no disrespect intended; as a child I was avidly both), behind which, it should also be admitted, is a measure of human guilt at having been the agent of devastation—the creation of the rarity—in the first place.[24] But if a life *is* a life, what then?

It seems that, as a rule of thumb—except where the *native* is also deemed *pest*, which in most cases is to say "interferes with human enterprise"—*native* outweighs *introduced*, that animals which are *not* to be found elsewhere are more valuable to us than animals which *are* to be found elsewhere, and that where *introduced* predates upon *native*, it's the predator who must be eliminated. A matter of national pride, we might wryly reflect, almost of national identity. But what do animals know or have to do with nations? We are all in this ark together, and if some of us (including *human* animals) are out of our own "natural" places (the word *natural* comes

24 I oversimplify (but see the following paragraph). If this is overkill (it is) then it's an overkill cats themselves are hardly innocent of. Feral cats have been calculated to kill over a million native birds per day, almost twice that many small reptiles, and an uncalculated number of rodents, small marsupials, etc. Surely, according to many, an excuse to kill as many feral cats as one can. But such appeal-to-the-animal (*they* kill, we should kill *them*) is weak at the best of times. It is *we* who have the perception and resources to do things differently. True, we have only our own ethics to go by, but we know what they are—know, for example, for all we try to pretend otherwise, that they don't include mass slaughter.

to look more and more like an ideological term, when one stares it down) it is not (except for humans) of our own doing. That we treat animals according to a logic we find within our own economic systems (think of—hyphenate—that word *livestock*) need hardly surprise us. Whether this truly means that one life is more or less valuable than another is another matter. It is *we* who have got the balance wrong and *we* who must find the solution, and the solution, although clearly we have not learnt this yet, is not to resort yet again to the killing that created that imbalance in the first place.

One could justify the concerns for preservation of a species, on the one hand, and the elevation of *native* over *exotic* on the other, with reference to the desirability of biodiversity and particular ecological balance respectively, but while each of these recourses has a certain logic, and in an undamaged and uncompromised environment could almost be considered principal, the environment is far from undamaged and uncompromised, and such truths, claims, or imperatives as those arguments (biodiversity and ecology) possess have to do battle with so many others—struggle, as it were, within an *economy* or *ecology* of likewise relative truths and imperatives—that we should perhaps consider that we are confronting a kind of paradigm shift in our valuations, or at least now find ourselves on a planet that is demanding one. Although it may seem outrageous to suggest it, it may be (for example) that our own survival is neither likely nor, as far as the planet is concerned, desirable. The environment and the shifting climate will determine—will make their "choices" as to—which species live through their crises; it is ultimately not going to be for us to do so. It is, after all, an old saw of human management that, when looking for someone to repair something, one should not trust the person (*homo omnicidens*[25]) who created the damage in the first place. But of course, as a race, a species, a top-order predator, we blunder on.

wandering into the sentences

25 *Omnicidens*: killer of everything. I thank Derrick Jensen (*Dreams*, 2011) for the term.

Postmodern Animals

There is one rat I call Clumsy. I don't know why I think of him just now, nor why, when I hear one of them losing their footing and tumbling down a wall cavity, I am so sure it's him. One day, when he thought my back was turned, I saw him make a dash from the garden into the alcove under the corner of the house where I keep my gardening tools and above which, presumably (I haven't been able to find it), there's a hole the rats can enter the underfloor by. Normally they scamper over the tools as quickly and silently as shadows, but—a little overweight, I think—he stumbled, fell flat on his face, and made no end of noise as he tried to clamber up, in his embarrassment, through the plant pots and buckets and bamboo garden stakes. Literally making a name for himself.

❦

"The animal" disrupts our writing. It demands. It stares at us and will not be explained (much as, now, as I write it, that "it" stares at and reprimands me: as I've said before, no animal I know is an "it"). *Charlie* stares at me, as he did only a moment ago, asking something, mutely, and trembling (was it the sound of Clumsy in the wall?). I am not just talking of that umbrella term, "the animal," and the fence it creates through what Derrida calls its intellectual violence, but, yes, also that. I am speaking of the violence of grammar itself, or at least its potential for violence—the way we can reach out, with it, to stroke a concept, a notion, a being, and find that, in and despite the tenderest intention, we have suddenly drawn blood.

Henry escaped, a week ago, to join the wild bush sheep, or at least what he must think are they. In fact (and the matter of *ownership* aside), they are our neighbor Geoff's, whom Geoff grazes on our swampy lower acre. Henry can see them from his paddock and longs to be with them. A herd instinct as much as a sexual. And one evening last week, at almost dusk, he made his move. I didn't realize it until, walking back from the cabin, I heard Jonathan bleating and looked over to see him standing in the center of the paddock, a clear sense of distress about him, looking down through the trees toward the swamp and then turning to bleat directly at me as if trying to tell me something. I went into the paddock and could see Henry nowhere, though in the bottom northeast corner there was a telltale depression at the top of one section of the wire-mesh fence. I know how high Henry can jump.

I alerted T. and she went down into the swamp on foot while I drove around to the lower boundary. It's dense scrub in there and she hadn't quite reached the spot by the time I arrived—had to be directed by voice—but I could see, very near the bottom fence, Henry and another ram in a butting duel, a ram fight, and that Henry wasn't getting the best of it. The sound of their skulls coming together was alarming. Like the sound of a blunt axe hitting the side of a large tree. As T. tried to approach Henry and single him out, I went to Geoff to see if he'd bring his van over—ours was loaded for the dump—and by the time we got back to T., she, Henry, and Charlie were in a huddle surrounded by a staring herd.

T. later said they all seemed astonished to see a human hug a sheep, let alone a dog licking the sheep's face. Henry, after T. had called him for a while, had actually come over to her as if for comfort—she said that he had been panting, was hot and *trembling* with his mixture of excitement, fear, and desire— and indeed it was much easier than I'd imagined to lead him (he actually allowed a rope!) through the bottom gate and into Geoff's battered blue van, almost as if he was glad to be being driven home.

T. and Charlie rode with Henry and Geoff while I came back in the car. Later, as we were waiting for our curries to re-heat (we'd abandoned our plan to make pizza; there'd also been the need, once we'd got Henry home, to shore up the bottom fence in the near dark), T. told me that Geoff had said all the ewes in that group were pregnant, and that they—she and Geoff—had talked about the lambs. She'd asked where he sent them to be slaughtered. He said that he was appalled at the thought of an abattoir—he'd once worked in one—and that he kills the lambs himself. He takes them somewhere they feel comfortable and safe, he says, and does it there.

Abraham, again.

❧

Am I any closer to an understanding of trembling? I don't know. This morning, watching the sheep through the kitchen window as the coffee rose, I was thinking there's a pattern in the way the day with them gets started. If I get up earlier they'll be grazing down in the paddock on the slope overlooking Geoff's, but by 8:30 on a clear morning Henry is usually under the cabin deck and Jonathan beside it at the fence, oblique to the house, each of them down on their haunches, quietly chewing over the morning's food, reprocessing it before sending it to a different part of their four-chambered stomach: something they won't do unless they feel secure and calm. And certainly Jonathan (I can't often see Henry at this point) *looks* calm. Then, a while later, if I come back for a second cup, it's likely I'll see Jonathan (not Henry, who's more likely to be standing off at the top of the rise, *willing* ewes to appear) standing at the fence staring up at the house, looking for some sign of movement—they can see us through the kitchen window—willing T. to appear (so well do they already know our routine). And then, should one of us come out onto the front or back deck, the *baa*-ing for attention—it's almost always Jonathan—will begin. Not every day, of course. Some mornings they are calmer, less anxious to summon us, but on others, particularly windy mornings, it's quite the opposite: the bleating begins and won't stop until we come down to them.

This morning I've come out to write on the veranda. A calm morning, sheep-wise. A short while ago, looking up from my diary, I saw that they were both together feeding out of the box of lawn-mowered grass T. left for them last evening. Contentedly, side by side, like loving brothers. Yesterday, however, it was different. Henry was in a foul mood. When T. put the box down and Jonathan started to feed, Henry butted him out of the way so forcefully and so often that T. decided to separate them—Henry had butted her aggressively the day before, and upset her considerably—and to bring Jonathan up to the top yard, out of Henry's reach. I watched through the kitchen window and saw Henry, wild with frustration again, trying to climb the fence to follow them. I was afraid he'd break through it, solid as I've tried to make it. And then, strangely, almost immediately, bleats of distress from Jonathan, and then from T. below, as Jonathan managed to scramble under the wire of the enclosure. Clearly it's one thing to be butted aggressively by Henry when he's in a foul mood and quite another to be separated from him.

All of which is to say that personalities have begun to emerge. Well, began, even in the first minutes of the first day. Even in the van as we drove them up, as so quickly they became "Jonathan" and "Henry-Lee." Naming was a part of it, but only a tiny part, a beginning.

How many of these traits are "natural," and how many— the bonding with T., for example—"acquired"? Are these even the right terms? Given freedom to do so, are Henry and Jonathan reverting to an archaic sheepness? A set of race characteristics that has been submerged and distorted by agriculture/husbandry? Although there are a great many who want to say that the wild sheep has long been bred out of these domesticated sheep, there is strong evidence that (s)he's always been there—suppressed, but there. Is that what's emerging here? Some of it? If so, it surely has to fight its way through and come to terms with—be altered by—the abuse that has individually happened: surely both Henry and Jonathan have been permanently altered, damaged psychologically as well as physically, by the removal of their horns, the docking of their tails, and (in Jonathan's case) the castration. Part of what we see as "personality," too (again not the right term: "individual character"?), is in the observer, and through interaction with the observer—habits acquired in and through and reflecting that interaction. A condition, overall, of what? A sort of postmodern animality? A fracturedness, if you choose to look at it that way, and a multipleness, absorption of things not experienced before, the animals—sheep in this instance, but Charlie's very much a part of this—in a state of *duskness* or *liminality* not all that different from our own. We are trying to address, challenge, think into the species barrier (though our progress could only be registered in baby steps, fractions of a percent); and *they* have no choice.

We are all in a strange new world. And most of them, of

course, in a slavery that severely represses individual growth and development, kills them in their blighted infancy, alters them brutally to eliminate those parts—horns, beaks, testicles, tails—that are inconvenient to their human manipulators, and in effect denies them any chance to acquire sheep/chicken/cow/pig culture or herd wisdom in the first place. The chances are that, if Henry-Lee or Jonathan ever experienced a herd life at all, it was only as infants, and in a herd comprised largely of infants. When and how, a few confused first weeks aside, could they have been taught to *be* sheep in the first place? What elders could have nurtured them, and from whence could those elders have got their knowledge? In all likelihood, true postmodernists, they've had to work it all out for themselves, put themselves together from a kind of experiential *bricolage*, make themselves up as they've gone along. Certainly, as one of its members, I know that any herd that Jonathan and Henry have is a motley crew indeed.

Henry-Lee

Herd Music

I've come down to the writing room at last, my own grass library, after weeks avoiding it, determined to get over some inner reluctance to sit down to just the kind of work it's been built for, and after an hour of settling in—listening for the ghost of the racehorse—have turned to look out the window onto what I call the Yellow Garden, after the zucchini flowers that were so abundant last year, and the marigolds I planted to attract the bees, though we might as easily have named it so for the old yellow piano which, rather than take to the dump (I've been told you can't even *give* them away) we've moved out there to let the wind and the rain play, a muted, elemental jazz, hoping the ferns will eventually grow through and spread out above it.

And the sheep are there, that's the point: the sheep are there. Not in the garden itself, which I've fenced off to keep them out (they love zucchini flowers, and marigolds), but on the grassy space around it with its profusion of ferns. I have put some jazz on the CD player, turned up the volume just enough to reach all the corners of the space, and pressed random replay for a constant background, more as a way of shutting out the world than of entertaining myself (just as my father used to do, I suddenly realize, with his classical music, of a winter Saturday[26]), though I don't discount the possibility that there's something in the constant accompaniment—the rhythms, the world of associations they subconsciously bring with them—that feeds the writing, creates an atmosphere that helps it happen. And the sheep are there. Henry and Jonathan are there.

It's a bit of a mystery that they are. Or was, until a possible explanation occurred to me the other day, wild and unlikely but I can't get it out of my mind. When I come down here to write or to do some other kind of work and *don't* put music on, as often as not Henry and Jonathan don't come. That is, they don't seem to appear simply because I'm in the cabin. But when I put music on—it doesn't seem to matter much *what* music; lately it's been, variously, Bob Dylan, Ofra Harnoy playing Vivaldi, albums of Keith Jarrett, Charlie Haden, Tord Gustavsen—Henry and Jonathan are there, as if something in the music draws them.

But of course they are herd animals, and there is no herd here. There are only the two of them, and while they, together with T. and me and Charlie and the ducks, rabbits, Indian mynahs, and the wagtails that have taken to riding around on Henry and Jonathan's backs, might be said make up a kind of postmodern herd substitute, it's not a *herd*, and it's quite conceivable that in the absence of such there is something constantly missing in their lives (another of those ethical dilemmas; they are rescue sheep, and to be in a herd of any "true" kind, while it may give them something they deeply need, would also most likely mean deprivation, neglect, exploitation, death: *instrumentalization*, I might say—for that is what T. calls it—if the irony wasn't so coarse).

26 W.G Sebald writes, intriguingly, of a passage he remembers in one of Freud's studies (but which I can find nowhere) describing music as "a gesture warding off paranoia," made—or played—to defend ourselves against "the terrors of reality." *Campo Santo* (Hamish Hamilton, 2005).

And I thought, then, suddenly, of the *music* of the herd, if music it can be called (but how else to call it?): the sound of hooves shifting in the grass or tapping on stone, the occasional bleat of a lamb, response of his mother, grunt or growl or call of a ewe or ram, the sound of snipping at grass-blades, coughs, throat clearings, nudgings, strokings as one sheep passes another, regurgitations, ruminant chewings, fartings, belches, sounds nearer and further off, all in all a constant, rolling concert, approximated—very distantly resembled, in a bizarre, post-something way—by the muted rhythmical under-music of whatever it is that I might be playing on the stereo system in my cabin, an aural equivalent of warmth, the ghost of companionship.

Is it too much to call these herd sounds music? I don't know. The other day as I drove in to town I heard a composition by the Californian sound designer Steven Baber made up of sounds from different parts of a bicycle. He could tune a bicycle wheel, he was saying, so that every spoke had exactly the same pitch. And there were mudguard sounds, tire sounds, handlebar sounds, frame sounds. I wonder what he'd make from grazing sounds, or Henry and Jonathan's wanderings through the scrub, their rummagings and settlings in the coop.

Walter Pater, in his essay on the school of Giorgione (1877), claims famously that all the arts aspire to the condition of music. He's right enough in some respects, but I don't think I'd put it quite that way, or at least would augment. In aspiring they are also returning, surely, to a place they have come from, rhythms rising from the body—the actual body, its breathing, its heartbeat, its walking—and the body of experience, memory, desire. When Rimbaud and Pound et al. dragged poetry away from its regular, repetitive meters it was to find, deep within their "free" verse, some very old rhythms returning. Aeolic rhythms, the rhythms of Sappho, based on the choriamb—strong, weak, weak, strong. A heart-like rhythm, or perhaps the hoof rhythm of the horse or donkey you are riding (instrumentalizing). Or, as I watch them now, of the sheep as they cross the paddock, *un*ridden, hooves following their own sequence, *a/c/b/d*, with its illusory contrapuntal *a/d/c/b*. Henry limping, having pulled a muscle again, a halting rhythm, three-four time.

If you listen there are rhythms everywhere. The relentless wall of cicada sound in the forest next door is actually pulsional, as if there were a conductor in there or they were in fact all, in their hundreds, singing the same song, coming to that astonishing moment when it all stops instantaneously, a whole forest of shrillness in a split second silent, the conductor having made a final, sharp, cutting motion, on the hottest of days, freezing everything. Or as if, in their ancient song—is it as simple as this?—they've just reached the last note, the last word, as all of them had known all along they would, together. Listening to the raucous chorus of the cockatoos the other evening—a flock of over a hundred settles each dusk in the tall pines on the other side of the valley—I realized that that, too, is pulsional, comes in waves, as they all raise or lower their voices together, or pause, now and again, for a soloist.

The sheep breathe sometimes very rapidly, their sides pulsing, heaving, when they have just run up the hillside, or just walked it on a hot day, or, I sometimes think, as they stand still, ruminating, when a thought passes—a fear, or some remembered or imagined excitement. One of their languages the language of breath. They come together, each looking slant-wise into the other's face, almost touching noses, go away as if they have received an answer, come to an understanding.

Cenesthesia, the sum of the sensations making up one's awareness of one's body, so many of which are of sound. And its extension into—*from*—the world about one. The *hum of existence*, I once called it, impressing my English tutor: the *modal drone of Being.* Silence hardly ever silence truly. That, and a fragment, from Pound's *New Treatise on Harmony*, that struck immediately as a truth and has stayed with me ever since— that no two sounds are inharmonious provided the appropriate interval has been found between them: the raucous cry of a crow, say, and the smooth, mounting shock of the whipbirds, which I had for so long thought the magically ventriloqual product of one bird alone but know now is the almost-as-magically synchronized product of two. Or the amazing, extended melody that magpies will sometimes greet you with as you cross their lawn. Or the extraordinary complexity of a swallow's song, when a recording is slowed dramatically down, so that within what seems to us a single chirp can be a whole sentence. Our hearing too fast. Or is it too slow?

With all this, why the need for supplement, "actual" music? Is there something we are *re*-creating when we create? What *is* the herd we are longing for? T. talks of the *ontological violence* we've done to animals, turning such biopsychosocial complexity into commodity. I wonder whether the culture has done an ontological violence to us, too, in separating us so much from the nature that molded us. The herd. Maybe one of the functions of music is surrogacy. That curious relation it has to the open mind, the deep body. Hear a piece of music at the wrong time and my jaws will tap it out (their *bruxism*); wake in the middle of the night and as likely as not I'll lie there going over obsessively one of the old songs, or a line or stanza of poetry, trying to get the rhythm just right, as if rhythm itself were a symptom, a hand reaching out, though whether to comfort or to warn me that I'm dangerously stressed I don't think I'll ever know.

Forget the fiction of the one day's creation, my opening gambit eleven paragraphs ago. In fact I've come back to this chapter/essay/thing/piece—*composition*—a dozen times, as I have every other chapter/essay/thing/piece in this book, over a period of three years or more, preoccupied with it but never leaving it much the wiser. We've had an Indian summer—climate change—but today it's cooler, overcast. I'm in the writing room and it's been going well—not this but another piece. I've come back to this chapter—is it to conclude it?—because I was sitting here, listening to some jazz again, high, thin, arctic, *boreal*, like the sound of distant gulls, when I realized that the gull cries in the music, the soprano saxophone, had merged with, become, the mixed chorus of the other birds, in the trees on the northern boundary—mountain lowries, tree creepers, finches, wrens—with no shred or skerrick of discord that I could hear. Then saw that Henry had come and was grazing just outside the door. I opened it—did he want to come in? was he drawn by the music?—but no; his eyes flashed an acknowledgment, the closest he comes to a greeting, then looked away. I pushed the door almost to, leaving it open just a centimeter in case he changed his mind, and turned back to the desk, to hear, after an appropriate interval, on the little wooden landing Vicki the builder made me just outside, a scattering of his black, shining pellets, like the gentlest rattle on a snare.

or the amazing, extended melody ...

Interlude

Early January, three months into our second year here, and a neighbor has died. Cancer, Geoff says. A nurse, who'd worked at an old people's home in town. Reclusive and eccentric; I can't recall ever seeing her. And Geoff's been looking after her animals, a small dog, a cat, a nanny goat. I'd seen the goat once, from the window of another neighbor, Sarah. She'd pointed her out, said she'd thought she was a compost heap at first, until she saw the heap move. She'd never met the woman either. She went over there once, she said, when she and Evan first moved in. The front door was covered with notices. One said I'M AN EX-USER, I'M OFF MY MEDICATION, AND I'M ARMED. Another read COME RIGHT IN! I'M ALREADY DISTURBED! "When I saw those," Sarah said, "I figured she didn't want visitors."

Geoff's already found homes for the cat and dog, but has run out of ideas for the goat. A female, he says, a Brown Boer. It doesn't sound as if he's tried very hard. We both have visions of him taking the easy option and giving her to Randall, down the road, for dog food (Randall, who has goats already, has huge dogs, and his own killing shed). No surprise then that T. offers to find this goat a home. She'll put a notice up online, she says, but needs to go see the goat, to take photos.

Geoff is only too pleased to let us try. "But don't turn your back on her," he warns. "She butts anybody who goes onto the property."

T. goes around and, of course, not seeing the goat from the street, goes in, and the goat is suddenly there, butting her. It is a large brown goat, she tells me when she gets back, with long, back-turned horns. I get no answer when I ask if she's been hurt—*She walks strangely,* is all she'll say—but later that evening, as I'm brushing my teeth, she comes into the bathroom and begins undressing to take a shower. There's a long, dark bruise on her thigh. When I remark in concern she turns to show me an even longer one on her back. I know for a fact that she doesn't bruise easily.

We decide that the goat needs a name. Geoff has no idea whether she has one or not. T., as usual, rejects my suggestions as too literary. Eventually she decides on "Molly," and composes a biographical sketch with the few details we have. That she's been a pet, that her human companion has died, that the cat and dog who lived with her have gone to other homes, that she's been living alone under the empty house. Nothing about butting.

It crosses our minds that we might not have any *right* to be doing what we're doing. Having been the "property" of the nurse, she's probably now the "property" of whoever inherits the estate. Geoff says he thinks the woman has a child or two, but can't tell us anything about them. So when, coincidentally, just two days after we've begun our search, a four-wheel drive pulls up outside the empty house and a couple of men begin to wander about, we go over and introduce ourselves.

Sure enough it's the woman's son. He hasn't known what to do with the goat, he says, and is only too glad to have us find it a home. He's asked some Middle Eastern friends whether they're interested, since he knows they eat goat, but they don't want a seven-year-old female. He can't see that anyone else would want it because of its butting. In fact we've just saved its life. He'd more or less decided, just that morning, to have it euthanized. It's called "Nut," he says—he refers to her only as "it"—and he's always hated it, for the way it's tried to butt him whenever he's come to see his mother. From the way he talks there hasn't been much love lost between him and his mother either. If there's any grief in the air it certainly isn't his. Through all of this I can't see Molly anywhere. It's only as we're walking off that I catch the glint of two eyes in the deep, cluttered shadow under the house.

Anyway, to cut a long story short—I could go on about what a prick the son is, but what's the point?—we find Molly a home, down at the foot of the mountains. It's going to be quite an operation. We'll have to pad the van, imagining an angry goat thrashing about in there—fill it with hay, use bales of it at the driver's end to protect ourselves from attacks from behind, and all this presuming we can get a belligerent, butting Molly into the vehicle at all without having spleens ruptured or hands shredded by her horns. There's an old door we can use as a ramp. With luck we'll be able to lure her in with lucerne. We call Geoff. He says he'll be happy to help load her—though he doesn't *sound* happy. He has a trick, he says, for calming her. He suggests music in the van, or the radio. She's probably used to the sound of the TV and might be soothed by the voices. Later that afternoon we bump into Sarah. She says she'll also lend a hand.

The night before the trip I go out after dinner to sit on the deck in the cool and the moonlight. I can hear the occasional *baa* from Henry or Jonathan, or from one of Geoff's flock a bit further down. Has Molly been bleating the whole time, in her distress, and no one hearing her? I listen now, intently, to see if I can catch any sound from over there. Sometimes I think I do but it's hard to tell one bleat from another, or a bleat of distress from any other kind. Perhaps they're all bleats of distress, from all over the valley. Later I drift off to sleep thinking about her, and how we'll get her to come with us. I devise a way we might *lasso* her, with a rope long enough for Geoff, at a safe distance, to hold one end and T. the other, to coax her to the van, sorry already that the process is inevitably going to traumatize her—and probably us—so much.

But in the end the loading's no trouble. We don't need the old door, the music, or the rope. At the designated time Geoff is already waiting at the curb with Molly on a leash. She's nervous, but also curious about what's happening. It's the first time I've been so close to her. I see straight away how misshapen her front hooves are. As if they've never been trimmed. No wonder she walks so strangely. After giving her time to settle and inspect the van, Geoff and T. each take a front leg and lift, while Sarah prepares to push from behind, doubtless anticipating a kick in the face, but Molly seems to be trying to make our job as easy as possible. And the fifty-minute drive is much the same. At first she shuffles about, trying to keep her balance, but then lies down and we hear nothing more. No butting, no battering of the van. It's warm. We have the windows down. Driving through the Yarramundi Forest we hear the clear, crisp *chink* of bell birds.

We're able to drive right into the new paddock. A woman, her husband, and their teenage daughter meet us. After a brief conversation we all move back while T. opens the hatch. Molly stands there a few seconds, allowing her eyes to adjust to the light, then steps calmly, almost regally down, looks curiously about her—at the two white goats, the single sheep, the horse in the next paddock, the three bull mastiffs observing keenly through an upper fence—and immediately, as if she's understood all along what's been happening and has been quite happy about it, begins to graze. The woman notices the hooves and says firmly they'll have to do something about them. The daughter goes off and returns with lucerne. The man rubs Molly gently between the horns and she lets him. I've envisioned all sorts of crises but there's been nothing so far and no sign of one now. After a few minutes we see no reason to stay. "You look after the gate," the woman says to her husband, breaking a kind of spell, "while I take her up to meet the others."

She waits for us to close the hatch, get in, and turn on the ignition, then, waving, thanking us, turns her back and begins to walk up the rise. Molly follows, calm and without bidding. Each of them high-stepping through the grass.

It's my birthday. Driving back through the Yarramundi Forest in the yellowing light we hear bell birds again, one after another, as if touched off by the shadow of the passing van. Their clear silver sound, in this moment, all the gift I could wish for.

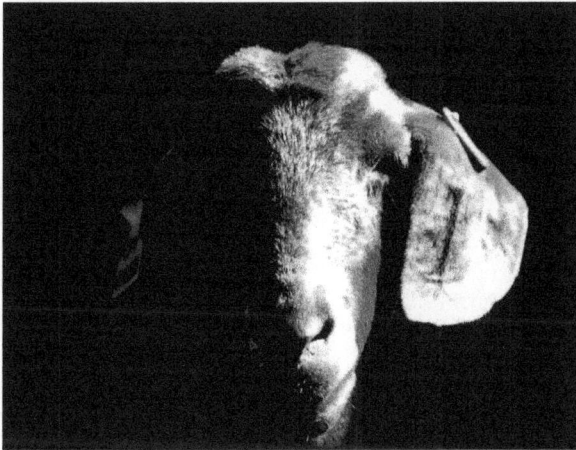

in the deep, cluttered shadow

Ghosts of Passage

I've called this chapter "Ghosts of Passage," but in truth *ghosts* seems too benign: *vampires* might be better, if they weren't so romanticized by popular culture. Perhaps, ultimately, the kinds of event I want to write about here are reminders that one can never reach the other side, or that one can only create for oneself the impression that one has done so by illusion and violence. If, as we human animals have done, you've assumed mastery over non-human animals, perhaps part of the price, the punishment, is that, however much you try to renounce or redress that mastery, it can never be shaken off, that it turns and faces you. That it *touches* you, leaves blood on your hands. I hypothesized, once, that a great many narratives contain, somewhere within them, a kind of pit or vortex where their key values confess or confront the paradoxes and abjections they've emerged from.[27] Henry's operation, Bobbi's death in Slovenia, and Orpheus' arrival which, however wondrous it's been, has also come with attendant dangers: perhaps, unexpectedly, before I might have prepared for it, this book has reached such a place.

27 "Dougald's Goat: Alex Miller and the Species Barrier," in *The Novels of Alex Miller*, ed. Robert Dixon (Allen & Unwin, 2012).

Henry

When he and Jonathan first came to us, I'd have been very reluctant to accept the idea of Henry's castration, and yet somehow it happened, somehow we were persuaded. And it nearly cost him his life. I don't know if the reasoning was good enough. It seemed so at the time. That should something happen to T. and me, and a new home need to be found for Henry, it'd be a lot harder to find a safe one for him as a ram than as a wether. As a ram he was a problem and a danger to himself, breaking through fences, scratching and tearing himself as he did so, even getting out onto the road sometimes. And if we could deal with the latter—were dealing with it, with new fences at several parts of the farm—we felt helpless before his desperate sexual longing, a longing which, amongst other things, made him a torment to Jonathan. Castration would be so easy, we were told: not as easy as it would have been if done when he was a lamb, but an uncomplicated operation nonetheless, with little pain attached—it could be done under full anesthetic—from which he'd make a complete and speedy recovery.

But something went wrong. It wasn't easy. It wasn't uncomplicated. And, I suspect, though he made no protest about it, there was a lot of pain involved.[28] When we picked

---

28 Not always easy to tell. Sheep are *prey* animals. When hurt, they tend to remain silent and may even do what they can to appear lifeless. Supposedly this is altruistic, an attempt, when attacked by a predator, to avoid calling the herd to them, and so into danger. I've seen Orpheus (we're coming to him!) get his hoof caught in fence wire and just lie there, where it's happened, making no sound, although his relief to be cut free at last was clear. Perhaps Henry's seeming to express no pain was something similar. But perhaps this is subject to other factors—trust, whether one is "accepted" as a member of the herd, etc. I've also had Jonathan come to me in distress, to show me where something—a stick? a snake?—has hurt his cheek.

him up afterward, coaxed him gently into the van, he was wearing a pressure bandage over his very large scrotum (Geoff, from the farm below, had remarked frequently upon how well-endowed a ram Henry was), but, although still a little groggy and tentative, seemed well enough. There were no problems by nightfall but the next morning—a dark, overcast morning—we noticed blood seeping through the bandage. Keep a watch on it, Mark said, a bit of blood is no real cause for alarm but if there's any sign it isn't clotting then we'd better have another look.

We checked on him through the day. For most of it he seemed all right. T. and Charlie went for their walk at three. At one point while they were gone, crossing from the house to the cabin, I stood at the fence and watched Henry. His bandage now seemed blood-soaked. But I was twenty meters away, couldn't see properly. The camera was nearby, on my desk in the upper part of the cabin. It has a zoom function. With luck I could take a closer look without disturbing him. And somehow, as I looked—he seemed so otherworldly, in the pool of light beneath the trees, at once so powerful and so remote, as if deep within himself—I took a photograph, and almost simultaneously realized, with certainty, that that remoteness, that deep self-containment, was pain. The taking of the photograph seemed suddenly, as it still does, an intrusive, shameful, selfish act, a betrayal, but perhaps it was also necessary, a lesson, to show myself something, break an old connection. Henry's gift, in a way, and he's been kind enough to keep the secret.

T. and Charlie returned. We coaxed Henry into the van again and took him back to the vets, left him there for observation. They put on a stronger pressure bandage and settled him for the night in an enclosure large enough to turn about in, but too small for him to be able to do himself or his dressing any damage.

At around 10 p.m., Colum, the principal vet, drove back to the surgery to check on him—he must have been more concerned than he'd let on—and found blood all over the floor. He changed the bandage again—tried a different kind—and thankfully this held until the morning. By then, however, Henry had lost so much blood he'd become anemic. When we went to see him—and bring him a breakfast of grains, fresh silver beet, slices of apple—the vets asked us to bring Jonathan in, to occupy the stall beside him, in case they had to do a transfusion. Henry and Jonathan might be blood brothers, like it or not, but they are not blood relatives, in fact they're quite separate breeds—the sturdy and powerful Henry is, ironically, a Merino, one of the less robust breeds (regardless of Australian legend), and the finicky Jonathan—I think of them as like Oscar and Felix in *The Odd Couple*—is a tougher Border Leicester cross (bred as a meat, rather than a wool sheep[29]). But apparently, for the first transfusion at least, a difference in blood type is not a major problem. Hopefully no more than one transfusion would be necessary.

Anemic. All we could think of were dark-green leaf vegetables. He and Jonathan stayed in there all week. Every morning and evening we brought them food—left lucerne for them during the day and overnight—and hand-fed them both: T. sitting in the enclosure with Henry, coaxing him with leaves and pieces of fruit, and I squeezing the same things through the grille to Jonathan. After two touch-and-go days Henry began to get better. We still don't know what had gone wrong—whether Mark, who'd done the surgery (but perhaps not upon so mature a sheep before), hadn't allowed for the way a ram lies, and the weight this places upon his scrotum, or whether (more likely?) Henry, that first night, had been too energetic, perhaps tried to get over a fence again, and

29 Which might explain his bottomless appetite.

re-opened the wound—but now at last it came right; within ten days we'd taken off his last bandage, an interesting and rather gruesome process, and three weeks later you might have thought (and been wrong) that he had no memory of what had happened. All of which does nothing to change the fact that, against all of our earlier resolutions, we'd brutalized him, and that, caught in the crosswinds that seem so much a part of this new territory, we'd not navigated well, had been blown back to an old and cruel place, and almost killed the very creature we were trying to help.

It would be easy to think, looking at him eighteen months later—his calmer character, his relative freedom from that aching desire, the way he is now an uncle, now an older brother, now a playmate to Orpheus, with what you could almost describe as a clear, open, untroubled affection for Being (and for T. in particular)—that we might actually have done the right thing after all, but I'm still not sure.

It's just as well we didn't carve some of our early resolutions in stone. We began this process of—I don't even know what to call it: stewardship? protection? attempted redress?—so naïvely, despite all the thinking that had gone before. But of course that had been thinking *about* the animal, *in the absence of* the animal. No one told us—who was there to do so?—that we'd encounter, almost inevitably, these pitfalls, dark holes, perilous places. As we open up to these creatures, as we apprehend more and more of their Being, or think we do, we're dealing more and more with lives no less complicated, painful, traumatized, or liable to trauma than our own—indeed we're dealing in most cases with lives that have been far more traumatized than ours are ever likely to be. We've developed habits, over millennia, of standing aside, having already cast ourselves as the decision makers, and where some of the decisions might once have been painful to make, we've institutionalized a good many of these, so that they're now just things that are routinely done. One *does* dock the tails of one's sheep; one *does* cut their horns, one *does* castrate the male lambs sometime in the first two months, one *does* remove pups and kittens from their mother, one *does* "put down" a suffering pet, still.

You'd like to think the more we allow their Being to awaken in our consciousness—the more these habitual procedures are examined, and *experienced*, removed from their institutional shell—the less we'd be able to stand aside, and the less stable that power relation would become. But it seems it's not so simple. The vast machinery of sequestration and relegation of the animal is such a relentless default position in our minds that even the most dedicated "animal people" are forever slipping. One might almost think these pitfalls, dark holes and perilous places are a kind of residual damage, from the original error, a scarring of the moral landscape that can never quite be put right—at least, not with the resources most people involved in that process of redress will ever have at their disposal. Ideally Henry would never have been castrated. Ideally he'd have been placed, with his beloved/beleaguered Jonathan, in a generous paddock somewhere, so well fenced that he could do himself no damage—or, yet more ideally, in which he could have a family of his own, who could live and extend, forever un-harassed by humankind. But instead it seems he's been doomed to be castrated, again and again. Even by me. I took a photograph of him, in his blood-covered distress, and now I write about him. For all the best intentions to use these things only to try to improve the lot of others like and unlike him, they are still castrations.

A few days ago I was talking with T. about Jonathan. She's been writing about *attachment* in human and non-human animals, and she was saying that Jonathan, in his needy standoffishness—that way in which he'll not approach you for contact[30] but will deliberately annoy you (by standing on his hind legs to eat the very last of the camellias, for example: we joke that he thinks he's a goat) in order to catch or hold your attention, and in the evenings, at the field gate, will *baa* for a half hour or more to be brought some lucerne—is a clear instance of insecure attachment, and we speculated as to what might have caused it. And once again, of course, we encountered the problem of biography. So many of these animals—rescue animals in particular—don't come to us with life histories, and in this sense (too) they're castrated, cut off from their pasts. The preservation of life histories is an effect of love. Abuse habitually *obscures* life histories. The animals themselves can't tell us, and until we can find the time and the way—for theoretically it *might* be possible—to trace Jonathan (say) back to his second-to-previous home, and the home before that, and ask those who've been in contact with him for whatever they know, presuming they cared to register anything, then we're left, as we have been with Charlie, with our own observations, deductions and speculations to explain his eccentricities and insecurities.

But enough. I took a photograph. And, when I care and dare to look at it, the bloodied scrotum, in the deep shade of that gloomy afternoon, burns like a coal.

Bobbi

Ironically, Bobbi, T.'s beloved dog in Slovenia (if that not be taken to signify ownership[31]), does seem to have come with something of a biography.

---

30   With some exceptions, as per note 28 above.

31   But how can it not be? Another mode of castration, the animal as property, yet the systems are all and always insisting upon it. An animal as property is a slave, no matter how comfortably, even luxuriously, he or she may seem to live.

Bobbi had been two or three years old when I was first introduced to him, so when we went to Slovenia this year, to visit T.'s parents again, he'd have been twelve or thirteen in calendar years. They say "dog" years are flexible and depend upon the breed. You can't rely on a simple 1-to-6 or 1-to-7 equation. Small dogs age, physically, more slowly than larger ones, and Bobbi was small—of a breed I tend to think of as Yugoslav corgi, though in fact I've no idea what it's properly called. But, either way, he was now getting old—by those formulae would be somewhere between 72 and 91 in human terms—and was showing it. People can seem almost ageless during their middle years but then, very often, it's as if they come to a point when something collapses and their age becomes suddenly apparent. Bobbi had reached such a point. In the early years he'd want to play fetch with his beloved plastic carrot, endlessly if you gave him the chance, but in the last few he'd slowed down, to the point at first where, after two or three fetchings, he'd just lie down and chew on it, and eventually to a stage where, if you threw it, he'd wander over, sniff at it and then lie down. This year no one knew where the carrot was, let alone when they'd last seen it.

In recent years, too, he'd put on weight, so we were surprised to find him now so slim. He'd been on a diet, and in the last several months there'd been a rule, since he's always been an insistent under-table waiter, that he not be fed tidbits from above. When we arrived I bent down straight away to rub his ears and under his chin, and immediately felt another reason. Lumps, under his jaw, far too large for mere swellings of the lymph glands from some infection—had to be, as in fact within a few days they were confirmed to be, lymphoma, malignant lymphoma. We had to wait two weeks for the results of the biopsies, Bobbi roaming around meanwhile with blue-green patches on his shorn places. When the diagnosis came he was given a month to live (strange wording, that, "given").

An operation wasn't an option, the cancer was too advanced, but the vet said she'd explore the possibility of chemotherapy. The medications would have to come from Croatia; she'd check on their price and availability. Not that price mattered, or matters. (I was unsettled to read, around this time, in the account by a famous essayist—and well-paid academic—of his relationship with his dog, so much about veterinary costs, not because they can't sometimes be very high, but because— and this may be just me—of the distance and power-relation this preoccupation seemed to signify. Would this writer have complained about his child's medical expenses? Or his own? His partner's? I don't know. Maybe he would.)

Bobbi, in any case, differed from Charlie, Henry, and Jonathan, in that his past wasn't quite the cipher theirs have proved to be. A few nights after Bobbi's death—I'm coming to that—T. gave me the story of his life, as much as she knows of it. It was almost as if she were speaking of one of her human cousins.

Just over thirteen years before, two dogs had appeared in the village, a smaller female—a bit larger than a corgi—and a larger male. The female came to live with T. and her parents, but the male soon left for parts unknown. Whether he was Bobbi's father isn't certain but it seems a strong possibility. The female, in any case, gave birth to four pups. One of them died at birth but three survived: Bobbi, a brother, and a sister. The brother went to live in a village twenty kilometers away, with one of T.'s uncles, and the sister went to live in Trieste, with the mother of one of T.'s old boyfriends. They soon lost touch with her, and the brother disappeared eventually, too, when another of T.'s uncles drove off in the first uncle's car, not realizing the dog was inside. He had an accident in town, and Bobbi's brother ran off—no one knows if he was injured—and, like his probable father, was never seen again.

It was a strange time for us all, this visit to the village. Some morbid spirit was gripping the house. Ten days before we left Australia, Nona,[32] T.'s grandmother, had had a stroke and had been taken to hospital, for days not really recognizing anyone and for weeks thereafter not making much sense at all, so affected in mind and body that the talk for a time was all of nursing homes, a funeral. And just days before we arrived—in fact we'd heard only the night before we left—T.'s mother had fallen over in the cemetery, of all places, hit her head, and gone into hospital with concussion. Three weeks after we arrived, T.'s father slipped and injured his back, and while we were waiting to hear the results of Bobbi's biopsies, the next-door neighbor fell downstairs and broke her leg and T. herself developed a lump in her tongue which for several days we all feared was cancer. And in a way Bobbi was at the center of it all. For those two weeks, as we waited for his results, he did not evidently deteriorate, indeed at times seemed markedly better. I wrote in my diary on July 20—we'd left Australia on June 1—that he seemed as lively as when we first arrived. "Various things to consider," I said:

> Firstly, when we arrived, Nona was in hospital, recovering from her stroke. Bobbi's days, when he's not out in the fields with T.'s father, are spent in the house, where Nona is normally the constant. A bond, and therefore, with her sudden absence, anxiety. He'd been alone, in this sense, and worrying, for a week before our return from Australia relieved things a bit. With us back, the house fuller, and T.'s trying to give him as much of a vegan diet as possible, he's seemed to hold on and even improve a little, the lumps not quite so evident. Nutrition may also be part of it. Vegan diet or not, he's apparently been throwing up

32 T. notes that *nona* is simply a word for grandmother and wonders why I capitalize it, but while I knew it was not her given name, "Nona" is all I ever knew her by and is capitalized out of affection and respect.

his food for a few months now. With T. back, and my love of *minestra*, he's been sharing my lunch, i.e., of soup, not of more solid stuff, and has managed to keep it down. It's a week or ten days since he vomited. He's getting attention *and* nutrition. It's now a week beyond the month he was given.

You can probably sense the hope there, but that's all it was. "Yesterday, however," the entry continues,

I felt his neck and the lump was bigger. He'd spent the day downstairs under the kitchen table—his old Nona-place—whether depressed or sick I couldn't tell, though I thought the former. If only we could tell him she's coming back today for good, and that the house is only so empty because T.'s parents have taken a last opportunity to get away for a couple of days on their own. But Bobbi of course has felt deserted again. No Nona, no M., no E., and although T. and I are here we're not enough. So, anxiety—two and a half days of it—and regression: it's that delicate a balance. But now Nona and M. and E. are back—two hours ago—and he's already more energetic. We'll see. A dog may be well aware that he/she is sick, but he/she doesn't *know* he/she has *cancer*.[33] At least not in the sense that he/she can get caught up in the narrative of

33 I leave this in because that is what I wrote, but I'm not comfortable with it. It sounds too much like Heidegger's "Humans die; animals simply perish." How do we *know* what a dog knows? I heard a story yesterday about a dolphin in an aquarium (loathed places) that had unexpectedly struck its keeper hard at a particular place on her back. As they x-rayed to make sure that the dolphin had done no damage, they discovered a large tumor in exactly that spot. To a human, this would be *coincidence*; to a dolphin it might be *diagnosis*.

it. Clearly love, presence, attention aren't a cure, but they're substantial factors. Cancer can't be easy for any creature, but humans add to it the *narrative* of cancer, and the narrative causes anxiety. What does Bobbi know? How does he know? I've watched him for signs. There are times he looks distressed, confused, in pain, times he comes and tries to bury his head in our legs as if asking for help or comfort, but times, too, when everyone's about and the heat's not a factor, when he seems happily unaware.

Heat *was* a factor. In fact we were in the middle of a heat wave, and after his initial relief at Nona and T.'s parents' return, Bobbi began more and more to show the stress of it, spending all day in the deep shadow under the table in the downstairs kitchen, not eating, not drinking, hardly moving. The night after I wrote the entries above, T. carried him upstairs to spend time with us, but he lay almost motionless. He'd raise his head in response to her coaxing, but it was difficult for him even to do this. On July 23, the night before he died, when T. and her mother brought him up again and set him down, under the full moon, on the cool paving of the balcony, he just stood as if disoriented or was in such pain that he'd gone deep into himself. Eventually he lay down, but not with any comfort and I think only because standing was so difficult. When he tried to keep his head up it swayed as if he couldn't balance it.

"Putting down" an animal. Why do we do it? And why phrase it like that?[34] Is it because *we* can't face their dying? It

---

34 I mean no disrespect to those human animals who find themselves in the often extremely painful position of feeling that this is what they have to do. I've been in that situation myself, as I'm about to explain, and have seen the agony of others in the same predicament. In a sense they, too, are victims of this ethically dark conundrum.

seems deeply disrespectful, somehow. An act of compassion, yes, to "put them out of their misery," but why *put*, not *help*? The language carries all sorts of assumptions, and as we hear it, learn from it, begin to understand *how things are said*, those assumptions infiltrate, mold us, taint our thinking. So that as we think or write about something that our civilization has repressed, something it's exiled (for it's not "the animal" alone), we have to scrutinize, unpick, even the language we use as we try to make our way.

While culturally we seem comfortable to *put down* an animal, we certainly don't do this to our friends, even when they want us to. In most countries we'd risk prosecution for murder if we did. It's as if we're engrained with the assumption, from long before Heidegger voiced it, that animals are incapable of the full, human-like *experience* of dying. That somehow their dying doesn't *mean* so much. To them, presumably, and certainly to most of us—certainly to Heidegger.

My judgment, in any case, demurred when a day later T. could no longer bear to see Bobbi suffering as he was (but no, that's not the right way to put it; language rides roughshod over our emotions and sensibilities, reduces them to stereotypes; some people have a far greater capacity for empathy, to the point, as perhaps was the case here, where they feel, notice, *experience* an animal's suffering to an extent that others don't) and decided to have him euthanized. Having watched him all morning, tried over and over to have him sip water, to come out of his stupor, she at last took him to the vet. I could have gone with her but didn't. Her mother was determined to go, and I thought so many people crowding into the small car would be too much for Bobbi, but also—perhaps foremost—because I'd done such a thing once before, and the experience had been so devastating.

In another life, decades earlier, I'd been one of the three human companions of another dog, Ike, a red heeler, who'd grown old, become almost blind, almost incontinent, and was suffering a kind of dementia. We'd find him, some days, stranded in a corner of the yard, staring at the fence, as if he didn't know where he was or how to get back inside. Before he'd become so bad we'd bought a house in the center of Sydney, and it was now time to move. We sensed—indeed had been told by a vet—that Ike was in his last weeks, that his quality of life had become very poor, and that the move to the new house, with its steps, its unfamiliar yard, its unfamiliar smells and sounds, would be too much for him.

I don't remember how much I was party to it—probably every bit as much as the others—but we decided ("it was decided") he'd be euthanized. My partner had raised him from a pup and couldn't bear to be present. We arranged for the vet to come to the house, so that Ike wouldn't have to suffer being loaded into the car and experience his last moments in a sterile surgery. On the day it was to happen, our last in the old house, my partner went out with our daughter and left me to be with him while it was done. I was to feed him small pieces of his favorite food—his appetite was still good—while it happened, and it was, as I understood, to be painless. A simple injection and he'd drift to sleep. That's not how it happened. The vet had trouble finding a vein in Ike's foreleg, and when he did, rather than slip gently into rest, my old friend spasmed violently, as if in agony, for several horrid minutes, fighting death with a strength I couldn't have imagined he had left in him, not in any way ready to go. I felt like a murderer, *was* a murderer. Never, if I could in any way help it, would I be party to such a thing again.

But Bobbi's end was calm, it seems, the kind of ending I wished Ike could have had: a needle easily and painlessly inserted, and a gentle drift into a sleep beyond sleep. They brought him home—he was still warm—and laid him in a box in the garage, on a bed of hessian sacks. T. has a mortal fear of being buried alive and was determined that he lie there until she could be absolutely sure he was dead. So he slept there, in this intermediate state, through the night and into the next morning. I went three times to see him, stroke him. Unlike any time over the past few weeks, he looked at peace and free of pain. Not that this in any way eased my conscience. There are some who'd say that if we're going to allow ourselves mastery over other animals, then we must take on, as well, responsibility for decisions such as these, and experience the guilt, shame, and pain that comes with them, if only because, for many, that's the only guilt they're likely to feel, in their relationship with non-humans.

Ghosts and passages. I was going to write of Orpheus here, but he's a world in himself (as they all are), and this chapter's long enough already. We'll meet him, I promise, in a couple of chapters' time.

deep within himself

Cicada Summer

Early October and uncommonly warm. September's average maximum was six degrees above the long-term average and it seems this month will be no different. In the chemist's, the greengrocer's, the hardware store, everyone agrees the climate's changing. It seems incredible so many politicians still deny it. The resources are running out and the "natural" world, such as we know it, is in severe distress, but, locked as we are into our rapacious selfishness—*omnicides*—we continue on our destructive path as if incapable of doing anything about it. I sometimes think nothing short of metamorphosis will save us. But how on earth do we manage that?

The cicadas, my almost-totem, are out earlier than ever. I wrote about them in my notebook three years ago and see that, then, they emerged at the *end* of October. It looks as if they've been fooled, too, or maybe they've just adjusted. After all, they've had millions of years to learn the signs. One or two meters down, feeling the earth warming. Or perhaps, since the larvae attach themselves to tree roots, they feel the spring sap rising.

The first I noticed was just on a week ago. Something stirred at my feet at the foot of the steps and flew-hopped a couple of meters, a large cicada in the grass, golden-backed, ruby-eyed, so striking and unexpected I went inside for the camera. Whether a *pisser* (female) or *drummer* (male) I couldn't tell (nor am I responsible for the schoolyard slang, but the names it's come up with for some of the species are wonderful: *greengrocer, double drummer, black prince, whisky drinker, yellow Monday*). Then, heading out for the mail, I saw a carapace, which of course I thought was *that* cicada's carapace, on the fence post by the letter box, beneath the cherry tree. Back split open, tiny white threads visible inside where it'd pulled itself free—where I like to think it had *removed itself from itself*—as if these had been ties of some sort, holding the carapace on. Veins, sinews, parachute straps: I'll have to ask someone. There's so much I don't know. I just have to take a step, some days, and there's another question.

Its: his? her? but how to tell?

The carapaces intrigue me. I remember staring at one, that time three years ago, on the top of a tomato stake, feather-light when empty, the image of fragility, and yet its claws—the *shells* of its claws—clung so tightly to the wood, in the ghost of the effort and agony of that separation from itself, that even the previous night's high wind hadn't dislodged it. I remember taking this thought in, turning it about, in my mind, before dawn the next morning, as if it were some image beyond itself, in that mysterious way the natural world and the human mind sometimes communicate, as if the one has informed the other. If we think we are anything other than *creature*—have crawled very far beyond it—we are kidding ourselves.

A book, a poem, is like that: the shell of something that has emerged, gone. Writers work hard at those shells, but when we finish them—a poem, a novel, an essay—there's a sense in which we're not there any longer. A cicada, I note, sheds multiple shells before the one we see clinging to the bark of a tree; and humans, too—human animals—have to shed carapaces, create shells, whether they're authors or not, if they are to mature. That can be agony, pulling oneself out of oneself.

I was wrong, of course, thinking the carapace on the fence post by the letter box belonged to the cicada that stirred by my foot at the bottom of the stairs fifteen meters away. Once they've emerged they have to sit a long while drying their wings. That short flight from my foot in the grass was probably that cicada's first, or very nearly. Hopefully it wasn't too premature, fleeing me, and no damage was done. Most likely the cicada from the carapace by the letter box was still up there somewhere, drying himself, getting used to his utterly new world, or had already done so and flown off, up into a tree, to begin calling for a mate.

Turning back toward the house I noticed a hole in the path I'd not seen before. A wolf spider, I thought, or trapdoor. But I was wrong about that, too. Of course.

The next day, out by the cherry tree again, checking on the fence posts I'd put into the holes I'd dug the day before— yet another of the fences in my attempt to negotiate our space with Jonathan and Henry—I put my hand on the top of a post to straighten it before the concreting, and something moved beneath my fingers, startling me. Another cicada. Luckily I'd done no hurt. Looking around, I realized there was a carapace on every one of the four fence posts. And the next day, coming out to attach the railings, now the concrete had set, dozens more. I counted twenty on the trunk of the cherry alone. Gone warriors, they seemed, a ghostly army, frozen mid-stride. I thought of the *Iliad*. Looking at the path a while later, where I'd seen the wolf-spider hole two days earlier, half a dozen holes more, and others everywhere I looked in the grass. *Cicada* holes, it suddenly dawned on me, exit holes, where they'd tunneled up from the roots they'd been drinking the sap from for however long it had taken them to develop, all together, to their final stage. Only now has it occurred to me that they are what I used to find, the larvae, in holes I dug as a child, and would kill them, having no idea what they were. How many thousands of creatures have I killed mindlessly like that?

Nymphs, the larvae are also called, and the adult cicadas, like the adults of other winged insects, *imagoes*, as if they're somehow not really themselves, have attained an idealized form.

Later I took a long, straight stick and tested the depth of the exit holes. Most were between twenty-eight and thirty centimeters deep. Clearly the depth of the root there. But apparently they can be up to two meters deep. The lines they make on the ground trace the root lines. This particular species of cicada—they're *greengrocers*—spend between two and five years in the larval stage. A way of avoiding predators, it's been suggested. A predator who develops a taste for them one year will go hungry the next, and hopefully the predator's life cycle and that of the cicadas will get out of synch. It makes sense, I guess, but no one really knows. Apparently in the U.S. there's a species of cicada that spends seventeen years in the larval stage. Even David Attenborough, in the video I saw, throws up his hands.

This morning, coming back to the house after watering the vegetable garden—planted early this year because of the warmer weather, though I have to keep an eye out (the eye of the skin, actually; you can tell from a particular kind of cold at dusk, *in* the dusk) for frosts—I found what I thought was a fresh cicada carapace in the grass at the foot of the birch tree. The upper part, however—the face—was almost black, whereas the carapaces have all been a uniform gray-brown like the soil they've just tunneled through. Shinier, this one, too. A nymph, dead now, who'd been unable to get out, unable to escape from itself. A victim of yesterday's high wind, maybe, blown from the tree (s)he'd tried to cling to in order to be able to pull him- or herself free. October is also a month of winds. I wonder how many others might have been blown from their trees? Perhaps, if they'd waited until the end of the month, they might have avoided this.

The wind blew all day yesterday—gusts up to 106 kilometers an hour, apparently—and long into the night. The mention of the 106 kph gusts was in a report of a terrible accident down in Sydney. A petrol tanker overturned on a steep slope, exploded, and slid down the road, igniting cars as it went. The wind was so strong there were fears the fire from the truck would burn neighboring houses. I thought of Les Murray's poem "The Burning Truck" and of things that come to change us. There were some acts of true heroism, apparently, when this truck overturned; doubtless there are many, witnesses or involved, who'll never be the same.

I went out just now to look again at the dead nymph. Surprisingly no bird has eaten it. Now that the un-shed shell has dried I can see the beginnings of a split—it's more like a scar—on the back. Cicada/*cicatrice*. "Scar." "Wound." I wonder. The female cicada lays her eggs in cuts she's made in the bark of a tree, producing a *scarring*. I could never do without language but it trips me up so often, particularly when I write about non-human creatures, that I've come to think of it as a kind of carapace of dangerous notions, something that will restrict us, hold us back, if we don't learn to use it with greater care and respect. Yet every now and then a word opens up, emerges from its shell, golden, or jeweled with emerald. You stop. Gaze. Wonder. As if some of the things we're looking for might be already there, beneath our tongue, secrets embedded in language testifying to an old covenant with the world that we've long ago broken.

At the beginning of this chapter I called the cicada my almost-totem. All I had in mind was my tinnitus, which can sometimes seem as if one has a colony of cicadas deep in one's head. Some days the sound is even and constant, some days pulsive, like a heartbeat, and some days—rare days—it's almost totally silent.

Why, today, are *those* so silent, those other cicadas, out there? Perhaps it's a matter of temperature. I've always associated the sound of cicadas with the summer heat. Two days ago it was warm and, after they'd dried and tried their wings, they burst into an incredible, penetrating roar of sound (Christopher Brennan's "torture point of song"[35]). Millions, it seemed, though it may only have been thousands, or just hundreds, since the greengrocer (*Cyclochila australasiae*) is amongst the loudest cicadas in the world. But then the wind came, and the temperature dropped. Although I know they're out there I can't, now, hear a single one.

When I think of cicada-sound, the questions only multiply. How is it they can all appear, or seem to, at the same time—cicada season, October—and have, apparently, only a two- or three-week breeding span, and yet their sound continues all summer? Are there generations of cicada all through the season, the October generation just the first of them? Does every cicada tree—for clearly our cherry is a cicada tree—have its own timing? How is it that sometimes the roar of the cicadas can be the one continuous, unvarying pitch, and sometimes have the rhythm of a heartbeat? Hopefully I'll find answers to some of these. Hopefully the Dark Ages will end and a Light Age return, but I am not holding my breath. Hopefully I'll come back, one day, and this—this writing, this book, this state of things—will seem a shell.

❧

---

35   From his poem "Fire in the heavens, and fire along the hills."

A Postscript (October 7)

Four days later and the cicadas are still emerging. A slow fountain, from the earth, as from themselves. When I began to write this chapter they were around me in their dozens; now there are hundreds: on the veranda boards—we have to tread so carefully—and in the grass, on all available wooden surfaces, even inside the house. The twenty gone warriors on the cherry tree are now sixty-three, and the Japanese maple turns out to be a cicada tree, too. I've seen a pair coupling on the dry, rain-eroded track beside the old carport. I've seen for the first time a cicada in the process of emerging from its shell, and seen another, just out, with his wings still unfurling. Shorter than the greengrocer, and a deeper reddish gold—but I suspect it's just that the wings are not yet full-stretched, and that the gold will turn to green as it dries. The schoolboy in me wants to call him a *golden goblin*.

Further Postscript (October 27)

Yesterday, in the train to Sydney, having drawn my attention away from the burned landscape, the smoke hanging everywhere low and close—for the bushfires have begun, driven by the October winds, day after day of sirens and anxious waiting (and how many millions of cicadas burned?)—reading, in *The Animal That Therefore I Am*, about the cicadas in Plato's *Phaedrus*.

The cicadas, Socrates tells Phaedrus, used to be men who, when the Muses brought song into the world, were so taken by it they could do nothing but sing. So—metamorphosis again—they were changed into cicadas, who, once they appear, supposedly (the Greek version) do nothing but chorus, not even eat. Given the role of witnesses, they report to the

Muses the artistic and intellectual achievements of men (in Socrates it's always men): of dancers, of poets, of philosophers.

So that's it: we are being *watched*.

Phaedrus, at this point in Plato's text, pauses to notice the sweet song of the cicadas. *Don't listen to them*, says Socrates, or they'll think you're lazy and have nothing else to do, and will give you a bad report. Instead continue to talk about philosophy and rational matters. Act as if you were sailing past the sirens, refusing to listen. Perhaps then you'll *receive their gift*.

A paradox, it seems to me: how can you learn anything from a creature to whom you refuse to listen?

Wild Ducks

We've turned the old swimming pool into a duck pond, or rather the ducks have. It's of little use to us, after all. Too small and the wrong shape to do laps in. We'd be unlikely to use it more than a handful of times each year, given the mountain cold, and a huge amount of chlorine has to be pumped in just to keep it looking like a swimming pool in the first place. The wood ducks, on the other hand, use it day in and out, snoozing by it during the morning, crash-landing in it after their afternoon flights, decorating its perimeters with their droppings (although strangely, now we've ceded it to them, they're keeping it cleaner: perhaps the chlorine was giving them diarrhea). And where there are ducks there are, each spring, very likely to be ducklings. Three last year, to a couple who lived in the forest next door (wood ducks nest in trees, though come to ground when they have a brood—at least until the ducklings are fledged), a three that was quickly reduced, by a particularly cold night, to two. We watched these two learn to swim, and eventually to fly. The family went elsewhere then. Sometimes it came back, with what we took to be uncles, aunts, cousins, friends in tow, though in truth it wasn't long before we could no longer tell who from whom— except the mother, who'd been aggressively protective, and who continued to utter a distinct warning call we'd come to recognize.

And this year ducklings again, in late September. To a different pair, quieter, timid even, whom we took (but what would we know?) to be first-time parents. Four ducklings, I saw at first, at the edge of the pond, but then more, five, six, eight! They seemed very young to bring to the pond—too small, as if just hatched, whereas last year's had been brought a few days older and larger. Not wanting to scare them we watched enthralled from the kitchen window, thirty meters away, as they were herded into the water, and then, with mounting alarm, watched them struggling to get out, those who couldn't manage it swimming around and around, more and more agitated and distressed. Surely the parents would help them up the two or three inches from the water to the pool's edge. Last year's parents had helped *their* brood when they'd had the same difficulty. But no, no help now. Then we saw, suddenly, something floating in the water, a bunch of leaves it looked at first, but we realized and went down as quickly as we could. Not one, but three, sodden and lifeless— there had been eleven, not eight!—and two others exhausted, struggling. The parents too confused, doing nothing to help.

T. scooped out the exhausted ones and we took them to the house. One died in her hand before we got to the door. The other we tried to place in a box on some soft rags, prepared food and got water for, though he far preferred to be held close to T.'s chest, did so well there that within twenty minutes he'd recovered enough to be reintroduced to his family. We took him back to the pool, only to find that while we'd been away the duck had taken her remaining brood swimming again— perhaps she'd had no say in it—and a fifth had died.

Thankfully by this time the pool had filled to the brim— we'd put a hose in the moment we'd realized what was happening—and all a tired duckling now needed to do was to step out. We watched, in any case, until there was too little light to see. The duck and drake, with their surviving brood of six, sat there, almost motionless, until pitch dark.

We were devastated. So many things ran through our minds. It seemed to us we'd been witness to—participants in—a tragedy, and we didn't know how or why. I felt somehow responsible, for not realizing that duckling season was upon us and having the pool brimming in readiness. An oversight. A stupidity. And I felt anger at the duck and drake for not helping the ducklings to get out, for bringing them there too early, for swimming them around and around so irresponsibly, as if purposefully to exhaust them. It even crossed my mind that, alarmed at the size of her brood and perhaps knowing she'd not be able to care for them all, the duck was deliberately thinning it down. I thought of Darwin, of survival of the fittest. Of "nature red in tooth and claw," that horrid line of Tennyson's (as if human animals are not also "red in tooth and claw," as any day's newspaper testifies). I went online to find stories of similar incidents, to see whether this was a regular occurrence, and yes, apparently it's not uncommon—though few animals can beat humans for filicide. I thought, with sorrow and sudden sympathy, that the duck and drake had simply been overwhelmed by what was happening, desperate to stop it but not knowing what to do, their minds numb with shock. But who knows what combination of these things it was, if any of them at all?

A tragedy. It was a tragedy. More than just *sad*, for example. Many things can be sad, but when there's a sense of overwhelming unfairness, abyssal failure, a massive blunder or error of judgment, it seems something else. I wanted to *call* these deaths tragic, if only to that perpetual interlocutor in my own mind, but I also felt strange about using the word, as if some category error or error of scale were involved. As if—in a kind of intrusion into the realm of the non-human of that

113

Shakespearean sense of tragedy as a term reserved not only for humans, but for humans at the top end of some very human ideas of hierarchy (kings, caesars, generals)—the term *tragedy* should be reserved for larger, more powerful creatures. Lions. Elephants. Whales. The cicada I'd see ten days later, still in its larval shell, trapped there because blown by the previous night's wind from the tree bark it needed as purchase to be able to pull itself free; a tiny body in the grass; and, a day later, under the letter box, the cicada half out of its shell that, as I looked more closely, I realized had likewise been trapped and died there, halfway through its metamorphosis. These things seemed tragic to me, too. Why then did I have such conversations with myself about the term? But the cultural discourse is speciesist, the very language is speciesist (the Word program, for example, at just this moment, tells me that the word *speciesist* doesn't exist: no point in asking it about *anti*-speciesism, then, or *counter*-speciesism, *trans*-speciesism), in ways that contain and constrain one just as a cicada's shell must constrain the larva—except that they, cicadas, seem to have found a way to get out, even if not every one of them succeeds.

A whole range of our concepts of value when it comes to animals seems deeply anthropocentric, all about *us* and not much about them. We value—to revert to the old binaries— the larger above the smaller, the fierce and powerful above the gentle (it's the lion who is "king of the beasts"), the native above the exotic, the sentient over the non-sentient (but of course define *sentience* in our own terms), the vertebrate over the invertebrate, etc. It is *we* who, out of the great weight of our own guilt, are prepared to sacrifice the lives (as if there were no other way!) of thousands upon thousands of a "common" species in order to preserve those of a handful of a creature driven to the point of disappearance by our own thoughtlessness and malpractice. How is it in any way defensible to call, as we are wont to do, the latter (the near extinction) a tragedy, and not the loss of any one of the thousands of lives taken in the attempt to avoid it? Is our compassion so feeble? Our problem-solving so paltry?

So much of our approach to the animal is a matter of opening, extending. If the word *tragedy* can't accommodate a drowned duckling or a cicada trapped in its own larval shell then we must ask not only how much of its use to us is as a tool for the defense of our own self-centeredness and misguided mastery, but also how many other of our implicit, unquestioned, and seemingly innocent assumptions might be the same. If the word *tragedy* trembles like this, *buckles under the weight of the animal*, how many other of our terms of value and classification, how many of our ethical and philosophical assumptions, are vulnerable in the same way?

As to the ducklings, I'm afraid the story doesn't end there. Two days later—we'd been in Sydney for a day and night—I was down at the bottom of the yard checking some old timber for a possible fence post. As, driven by some impulse I can't recall, I went behind the woodshed to a small clearing there, I felt eerily—a feeling *ap*prehended before it was *com*prehended—as if I had strayed into a place, a pool, of great sadness. The duck and the ducklings were there, huddled together so closely I couldn't count the latter, and the drake lay strangely on the ground, flat on his belly, or so it seemed to me: not dead—somehow, instinctively, I knew it wasn't that. It was a glimpse, a glance only, but I had an immediate and guilty sense of intrusion, trespass. I thought—but I was just grabbing for a human comparison—of homeless refugees, people after a natural disaster. In retrospect (two years later, re-reading this) I think of it more as something opening before me, a portal, a *yawning of being*, a finding myself on the edge of a kind of psychic well.

The explanation—a *possible* explanation—didn't come

until the next day. The night before we'd left to go to the city had been a very cold one in the mountains, just 1.2 degrees Celsius. And the next morning we'd been so busy preparing to leave we'd not had a chance to check the ducks and ducklings. It wasn't until two days later—the day after my encounter above—that we saw them by the pond and were able to count. Four ducklings now, not six, and no amount of counting would make up the number. It might have been a fox, for certainly they're about, but I'm fairly sure it was the cold. The family there, like that, seemingly homeless, seemingly refugees, could quite well have been just that, homeless. If the ducklings had died of cold, then they—their bodies—would most likely still be in the ground nest. What choices did the family have? Move house? Make a new ground nest (or whatever it is that they sleep in before the ducklings can fly: I think this family were holed up under an old sheet of galvanized iron in the forest next door)? Go back the next night to sleep with the dead? They could have dragged them out, taken them some distance away, but somehow, from what we'd seen, this couple didn't seem to have that kind of initiative—or perhaps, in their grief, just didn't have it in them.

But all that is supposition, and what to take from it? They say we humans are language creatures—as a longtime teacher of literature, I've asserted this repeatedly. But we are also *creatures, before,* and *under* language. Language may be indispensable to us—as I imagine it is for a vast number of species—but it's not all there is. When I walked into that pool of deep, inexpressible sadness behind the woodshed I experienced something much older than language—and, I suspect, of incalculable use to the beings we share our spaces with.

And where do the ducklings fit in, in all our strange, confused, and human-centered systems of ethics and value? Well, for a start, they're *wild* (wood) ducks, and *native,* and aside from treading on the occasional seedling (and eating all my radicchio ...), not much of an impediment to human endeavor. Three points in their favor, one would hope, though clearly not in the state of Victoria, where many, many thousands of them are slaughtered every year in the name of sport.

Our local council has a policy of forced removal of non-native ducks from waterways in its jurisdiction. See a mallard, for example, and you're supposed to report it. For a time, two summers ago, a lone mallard drake—a refugee of some kind, perhaps a widower—came to the big pond in the wild park. He seemed to appoint himself guardian babysitter for the many native ducklings there, and for weeks, as far as we could tell, did an exceptional job. Then I guess someone reported him and he disappeared. A loss, it seemed to me, to an environmentalism too narrowly, humanly, selfishly defined.[36]

I was going to end this chapter there, but just opened the window of my writing room to let out a fly and caught again the whiff of smoke. Two weeks ago an irresponsible action of the Australian Defence Forces (they've apologized, but what help is that?) started, near the town of Lithgow, a bushfire that has since destroyed numerous properties—a "tragedy," as this of course has been described (the word has been used far more liberally concerning the loss of nearly two hundred homes in a second fire started on the same day, near the town of Springwood)—and over 58,000 hectares of bushland, much of it in the Greater Blue Mountains World Heritage Area. I don't dispute that the loss of one's house and belongings is tragic—we've spent much of this same period trying to protect our own—but cannot (I've been sitting here trying) find words for the impact upon non-human animals. The bushfires here in the mountains caused no loss of human

---

36 But who knows? T. tells me there's an alternative story there: that someone rescued him before the council could get to him. Let's hope so.

life that I know of—the headlines are saying "not one life lost"—but if we allow for only one non-human animal per hectare we are speaking of 58,000 lives, and of course there are many, many more than that one creature living in each 10,000 square meters of bushland. The deaths of marsupials alone must be in the many hundreds of thousands. A tragedy? Beyond reckoning. Unwept, unburied; the countless injured and traumatized survivors generally not even seen, not even looked for.

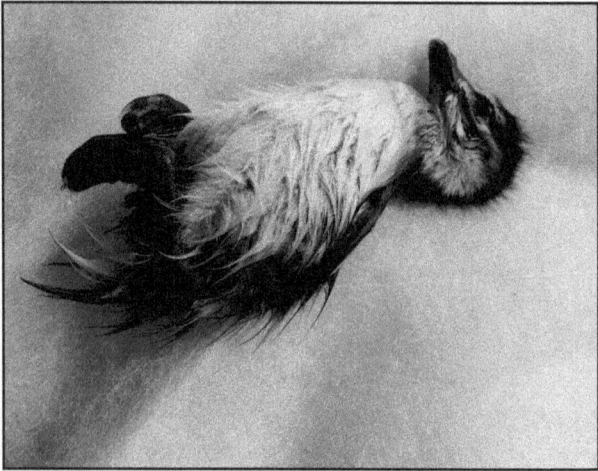

too small, as if just hatched

Orpheus

Maybe there was more to the choice of name than I realized. With his small horns, tight against the skull, and the waves in his wool (I almost said *curls*: are they just his youth, his "baby" wool, or is his wool different from Jonathan's and Henry's?), Orpheus is a young Pan, *lyric* without sound. I think of the young Van Morrison, the young Bob Dylan, though at first, I suspect, the name came to me because of the similarity in sound to *orphan* and their obvious shared root—as ordinary as that.

He'd come from death in a double sense. Not only had he been found, a three-day-old lamb, beside his dead mother (does he still carry that around, deep in his mind? he must), but in just another day, if he hadn't been spirited away, he'd have been "euthanized" as excess to requirements on the university farm where our friend, a vet student, found him.

She'd called us—if she could rescue him, would we take him?—and there'd been no question. But she'd had an exam to do and couldn't bring him up herself. She took him first to Sydney, to stay overnight in the house she was sharing with friends, and the next morning one of those friends drove him into the mountains. He came with a packet of nappies—was wearing one (size zero) when he arrived—and a Vegemite jar of formula marked "Lamb Powder." He weighed little more than a kilo, was barely thirty centimeters high. When his overnight friends had gone, we took him down to meet the boys at the gate (he was far too delicate to be set down amongst them). After a few minutes sniffing up at their huge noses through the wire, he settled into a patch of thick grass in the corner where the gate meets the cabin deck, so that he could watch and be near them as the afternoon wore on.

He slept in a nest T. made for him on the floor on her side of the bed. Once or twice during the first nights he'd wake and she'd gentle him back to sleep, but soon he was sleeping through. The nappies worked well initially but before long they were getting so full by morning they'd fall off as soon as he got up and began to trot about. If they hadn't done this already we'd take him into the bathroom, put him into the empty tub before we took them off, then wash him with warm water from the showerhead.

From almost the moment he arrived he grazed in the yard, or at least went through the motions. We noticed quickly that he was chewing *at* a bit of grass or stalk of hay or lucerne without actually swallowing it, and we'd only let him do this—"graze"—when the boys, huge by comparison, were safely on the other side of their fence, so that they wouldn't jostle him. They were as curious about him as he was about them. After a while we began to leave him out there, chewing, and would come back to find him curled up again by the sheep gate, watching Henry and Jonathan on the other side, and them, now and again, coming over and nosing him through the mesh. At some point—it can't have been more than a week after he arrived—we found that his poops had gone from semi-liquid green to the firm, tight pellets of a creature actually processing some of the grass.

We looked for signs of grief and stress and although they were there—in the first days his favorite places inside seemed to be the central heating vents, most probably for the warmth but we imagined him using them to communicate with his mother in the underworld—they seemed to vie with an intense, almost ravenous curiosity. He'd curl up beside one of the vents but, rather than sleep, seemed determined to watch us, whatever we were doing, late into the night. We'd see him, sometimes, struggling to keep his head up, though whether he did this because he was afraid of missing something or afraid of sleep itself is hard to say. Perhaps he wasn't afraid of anything at all.

The lamb powder ran out quickly and we had to find something else. He might be getting *some* nourishment from the grass and lucerne but it could hardly be enough. Supposedly he needed five feeds a day. As vegans we resisted the idea of another lactose-based compound. Sure, it's helping some animals, but it's exploiting others in order to do so, no less than human tastes for cheese or cow's milk do. So— since we ourselves find it adequate, and (we'd run out at the beginning of a weekend) had few options anyway—we tried nut milk, which we "make" ourselves. Almond seemed to be his preference, certainly he wasn't in any way reluctant to drink it, but almost immediately he developed diarrhea and, well, ceased to thrive. On the third day we did some late research only to find that almonds are not good for sheep—in fact that we were virtually poisoning him. Human babies can be lactose intolerant; what do *their* mothers use? We found an account on the web of someone in Queensland who, at the age of seventy, had suddenly found himself with a ten-day-old lamb to rear, which he'd done quite adequately, it seemed, with a commercially available soy-based infant formula. We tried this and Orpheus loved it, but his diarrhea took on a slimy consistency which led us to the vet and the discovery that he now had a condition called *scours*.

Mark gave us a tin of what he assured us was the *real*

"lamb powder" (I won't give the brand), and some medicine for the scours, and Orpheus improved almost immediately. Ethically, since this formula was of course lactose based, we were uncomfortable again, but could we endanger Orpheus any further for our own principles? When this tin ran out we went back to the vet, only to find that that had been their last; we'd need to wait two weeks for a new shipment. I telephoned around, found another vet who had some, and drove to a neighboring town for it, but was dismayed by the price. At this rate—a can a week—hand-rearing a lamb was going to be a very expensive process. We didn't begrudge him, but how did farmers manage? By going to the produce store, evidently, for there we found a fifteen-kilo bag, from China, for the same price as about one kilo of the tinned formula. This only intensified our ethical dilemma—call it a back-down—and we gritted our teeth every time it came to mind. If only ethics operated on the one plane, but they can seem stacked sometimes, almost three-dimensional, tougher to align than a Rubik's Cube.

Perhaps that's why so many people set so many ethical considerations aside. We've had a cancer scare—all clear, according to the biopsies—in just the week before my writing this. I can't see anything worse than losing the partner it's taken two-thirds of a lifetime to find, and my feelings for whom, to say nothing of admiration, are beyond any adequate expression. Were the biopsies to have shown malignancy, and if it were up to me, I would, I think, use any treatment available, regardless of its origins and the story of its development. She, on the other hand, not concerned how many sleepless nights she gives me in mere contemplation of the possibility, has vowed she'll never use chemotherapy, or any other treatment tested on animals. No amount of pleading that she's too valuable *to* animals to endanger her life by refusing drugs tested *on* them will change her mind. She is, in this, far stronger than I.

I seem to digress but I don't think so. Live with rescue animals and there's hardly a day without its drama, its wonder, or its ethical challenge.

Take space, for example.

Clearly Orpheus wouldn't be able to live his entire life in the house with us. He'd be better off, in every respect, with Henry and Jonathan, the only herd as yet available, and we were concerned from the beginning about how to phase this process. As early as the second or third week, T. moved his sleeping quarters from beside the bed to a part of her study, sectioned off with chairs, bookshelves, and chicken wire, that we came to call The Corral. He could have food there, to eat during the night, for by now, although still bottle-fed four times a day, he was also eating lucerne; he could have water; he could have a more comfortable bed; he could have a space he didn't have to share with Charlie. And, although it was only another couple of weeks before he was big enough to scramble out in the mornings, looking for company, he seemed happy to have this area of his own, indeed some nights only too pleased to be ushered into it. I bought some fake grass from the hardware store that we thought he might use for his toilet. Horrible plastic stuff which he rejected immediately. Instead he chose to pee into a small dog basket we'd initially given him to sleep in—a leftover from one of Ellie's visits, which she'd rejected for some reason. T. covered it with a plastic garbage bag, making a bowl of it, which he then used, quite neatly, night after night (his pellets were another matter).

In the corner, because we could think of nowhere else to put it, we'd left a small cabinet—it used to be a bedside unit—and covered it with a foot rug. He'd climb onto this most evenings and settle himself on top, watching out over the room while T. worked. Hour after hour, a vigil, head held high, wide-eyed. When he was ready to sleep—we'd see him fighting against it, as I've said, almost as if he was afraid of it, eyes slowly closing, head declining, then bouncing open, lifted high again—he'd at last get down and curl up on the old pillow we'd given him, but this was often not until one or two in the morning (T. is a night owl). And just as often he'd be up there again, a few hours later. I'd see him when I crossed the corridor for a pee at 5 or 6 a.m., staring wide-eyed at me in the pre-dawn light, as if his cabinet were a tussocky rise and T.'s study a field of grass. For it's like that. You get up, no matter how early, and over and again you'll see them there, lying at the top of the paddock, looking out as the sun rises over it, chewing thoughtfully, as if they've been up for hours, as of course—sheep don't sleep much more than four hours in twenty-four, and most of that during the day—in all probability they have.

That he'd bonded to T. is without question. I'd even have to hold his favorite bottle—an old beer bottle with a rubber teat—*exactly* as she did, in order to get him to drink from it. But he'd bonded to Charlie as well, and I think Charlie to him. After all, and although this changed in not much more than a fortnight, Charlie had initially been a fair bit larger. He's also a generous and protective dog, once he's accepted someone and the boundaries have been clearly drawn. Very soon they were both running to bark at the postman. Very soon Charlie was grooming him, as he will many white, woolly canines (poodles ...). Very soon, too, Orpheus Pumpkin (yes, "Pumpkin": T., rejecting "Orpheus" as too literary, had called him Pumpkin almost from the start) had developed a taste for the pasta, vegetable, tofu, and seitan mix Charlie lives on, to the point where, when they came in from an afternoon outside, he'd race Charlie to the bowl.

But it couldn't last forever. At some point he'd have to live in the coop with Jonathan and Henry. Needless to say the original plan of hand-rearing him and trying to find him a home somewhere else hadn't been mentioned since the earliest days; he'd grafted onto us, or we onto him, more with every sunrise. But his developing hooves were getting louder and louder on the wooden floor, the smell of his urine more and more acrid in the mornings, and the barrier around his corral seeming more and more like a token gesture. Indeed after the first few weeks he was perfectly capable of getting out of it whenever he wished, though never did so until one of us had woken.

A brief rumination:

Sheep are not meant to live indoors, I was just on the verge of writing. But with that word, *meant*, a whole new issue arises. A pod of thought, you might say, breaks open, spills.

We don't know what is *meant* for any of us. The very notion of *meant* implies an *agency*—i.e., some one or thing to do the meaning, have the intention—and our guesses in this regard have been flagrantly self-interested (a taxi driver a few months ago, upon hearing we lived with "rescue" animals: "But aren't they *meant* for us to *eat*!?"). Moreover, and perhaps paradoxically, the word "meaning" itself—a noun, as in "the meaning of the word *meaning*"—is also a *gerund*, a noun-verb, having nothing to do with some past determination by some being or other concerning our or any other creature's *purpose*, and everything to do instead with our continuing attempts to understand the immediate circumstances of our own being—in other words a *process*, something we *do*, rather than something we receive as a *fait accompli*.

Sheep, to return to what I was about to say, aren't *meant* to live indoors. They're not *meant* to sleep beside human beds. They're not *meant* to be corralled in small partitioned areas in a human animal's study. While they may enjoy the warmth of central heating, the comfort of a fresh blanket, the security and the company, there is, conceivably, as much or more of what they need that they're deprived of in such circumstances: the herd-being, for one thing, and the source—or the option to reach, at need, such a source—of the food, grass, for which their four-chambered stomach is best adapted.

This may change, of course. It may itself be part of ongoing negotiations as we *mean* our life with them, or they *mean* theirs with us. We live, as I've said, human and non-human animals alike, in a postmodern world, postmodern and (although this, for non-human animals, is still embryonic, not yet even in its infancy, and only for those who've escaped the machine) also postcolonial, and on both sides (i.e., human and non-human), it may be, will experience radical ethological and ethical change. Any "negotiations" entailed in this process may in so many ways be inevitably one-sided, but, for we human animals to do our best by and through them, these negotiations must be premised upon *as much as we can know* of the non-human animals concerned. At this point such knowledge, too, is still in its infancy.[37] We may have "known" them enough to keep them within a prison of human knowing, but we have not

---

37 Anything to avoid the disappointing mistake (if it *is* a mistake, and not a violent and willful exclusion) made by Heidegger in *The Fundamental Concepts of Metaphysics* (1938): "We keep domestic pets in our house with us, they *'live'* with us. But we do not live with them if living means: *being* in an animal kind of way. Yet we *are with* them nonetheless. But this being-with is not an *existing-with*, because a dog does not exist but merely lives. Through this being with animals we enable them to move within our world. We say that the dog is lying beneath the table or is running up the stairs and so on. Yet when we consider the dog itself—does it comport itself toward the table as table, toward the stairs as stairs?"

No, one would answer: why should it? How can we take seriously a non-human animal's "inability"—"inability" and disinclination—to relate "properly" to furniture designed for a human animal as demonstrating that that non-human animal does not "exist" but merely "lives"? Would Heidegger accept (as some speciesist dog-philosopher might aver) that his inability to determine a conspecific's state of health by smelling the traces of that conspecific's urine on the base of a tree-trunk meant that he, Heidegger, "does not exist but merely lives"?

known them—or, if some of us have, over the millennia (I think some shepherds must), the culture hasn't encouraged us to leave much record.

How on earth to embark upon such negotiations? Well, for a start, *options* can be offered. We must see what, of *our* spaces, the non-human animals with whom we would negotiate, desire. One thing I've come to know about the ethology and ethics of sheep, for example—one thing that it seems to *me* I've come to know—is that they have a great interest in fences, and that this interest spills over into the conceptual fences we try to set up, the prohibitions, in places where no actual fences are. If an actual fence is there in order to prevent sheep from reaching some thing or place—a particular tree or vegetable patch, say, or area of grass—then they'll be most interested in reaching that patch or tree or area of grass. They will, for example, in any new area to which they are introduced, go straight to the fences enclosing it and attempt to graze, first, not the grass within that area, but whatever grass they can reach (by straining of necks, getting down on knees, bending of wire) on the *other side* of those fences.

So, too, if they know, although no fence exists, that they are not to eat of a certain tree (!) or stray into a certain garden, they'll make a point of trying to eat from that tree or making for that garden. They ascertain that such a tree or garden is out of bounds by the behavior of the human animals who seem to think they have some sort of authority over them (sheep and trees/gardens alike)—behavior which may take the form of shouting ("Hey! Get out of there!"), actual physical movement (shooing, pushing, "warning": T. squirts jets of water at them from her ancient water bottle), or, as also in our case, the barking of a self-designated sheepdog/foreman (Charlie) who sees that the sheep are engaging in a behavior that, were a human present, may result in shouting, physical discouragement, etc.

Though even here, as to motive at least, we must be careful not to presume too far. Sheep may like to go to such trees or eat from such gardens because they dislike proscription and are making a point by deliberately breaking the "law"; they may do so because those particular trees or that particular garden are especially tasty to them; they may do so because they wish to elicit from their human companions the kinds of response that these modes of "trespass" elicit, i.e., see this as a kind of game; they may have reasons that are a combination of these, or they may have other reasons entirely—certainly reasons that haven't yet suggested themselves to me. But one thing that does seem apparent is that, once these restrictions are removed, the possibility of choice exists and seems to be taken. With no prohibition, for example, the tree may be left alone (that particular tree, at least: others may still be chosen).

All of which is simply to prepare for some talk of human spaces, for of course the first concern, when one writes of negotiation, is that non-human animals will invade such spaces, and must accordingly be kept at bay. While it's true that Henry, in his early days with us, finding the three-step entrance to the veranda blocked, took a flying leap and smashed through the balcony rails, then ran along the veranda and into the house through the open French doors, it's also true that, once he'd looked around inside, he left, having satisfied his curiosity and decided, at least for the time being, that it was not for him. So, too, with my writing room, the door of which, if the sheep are about, I will often leave open so that they can come in, as they clearly like to do, whether just to say hello, as I think of it, and check out the space, or to shelter a while from the heat or the rain, to sip from the water bowl in the low windowsill, or perhaps to tell me that they've hurt themselves, and to see if I can do anything about it. They are particularly interested in *re*-arrangements. Of late, for example, I've been building, into the upper room of the cabin ("the Library"), a small toilet/shower space—a W.C.—and they've come in quite frequently to inspect. But the stairs[38] from one room to another worry them, as do the stairs to the veranda up at the main house. Provided they're not *forbidden* from doing so, it seems they'd rather not use them. Amongst other things, human spaces, *non-sheep* spaces, can be *dangerous*. Henry and Orpheus Pumpkin have each taken a fall from the veranda stairs, and Jonathan has tumbled down the three stairs from the cabin kitchen into the writing room. And boring. All the books in these rooms! *Leaves of Grass* doesn't smell of grass at all. *Antic Hay* doesn't smell like hay. There is no grain in *Silo*. *A Body of Water* is undrinkable. *A Million Wild Acres* is barely five centimeters wide. By the same token, one could get annoyed by the way the sheep, when one is carrying something from the house to the cabin, or the car to the house, or one part of the yard to another, will come up and insist on investigating, or one could simply build the likelihood of such investigation into one's movements, *showing* them what one is carrying: a roll of masking tape, a can of paint, a box of papers, one's computer, one's cup of coffee (which isn't to say that, unless one's prepared to share, one should carry bread or fruit or leafy vegetables when the sheep are anywhere near). Doubtless our own relations with *them* would be all the smoother—and better informed—if we felt the same kind of curiosity.

But I was speaking of Orpheus, and of his double weaning—the weaning from his bottle (from five times a day to four, to three, to two ...), but also from his human spaces. Some animals, supposedly, will kill, or ignore to the point of starvation, creatures of their own species who have upon them the scent (to them it may be a stink) of the human. We didn't imagine that Henry or Jonathan would kill or consciously

---

38   See my previous note (37) on Heidegger.

harm Orpheus once he was introduced more fully to their spaces, but neither did we think this introduction would be easy. There were their feelings to consider, and we could only guess at what those might be: jealousy? resentment of the intruder? And there were his own. Of banishment, perhaps, or betrayal: his first mother dying on him, his second, surrogate, human mother evicting him.

We had to work out transitional arrangements: to slowly introduce him to the outside night, to longer and longer periods without our company, to longer and longer periods— during the daytime, at first, since he'd have to be a lot larger before we could risk him sleeping with them—with his moody and eccentric uncles. A gradual weaning from human to sheep spaces. We'd have to be very careful as we did so. There was a fox about, and a pack of dogs. Clearly, too, there was a *psyche* involved. We had to do all we could to ensure that Orpheus Pumpkin did not see weaning as rejection. In effect we—though T. did this far more than I—had to *accompany* him, as far and as best we could, like psychopomps, from one world to the other; retreating, yes, to our own, but (hopefully) only once having made that link, established that conduit. And, of course, in the process of leading, we were being led.

We were confident Orpheus's desire to be a sheep would prove greater than his desire to be a human or a dog, and that, left to it, he'd eventually wean himself. We were inclined to *encourage*—he might need some nudging before he got the idea—but certainly not to push. Beneath the house is a laundry which, needing a second bedroom for guests, we'd turned rather crudely into a human sleeping space (cum storage room). Now, for a time, it was to be his. The old sofa bed we'd installed there very quickly became Pumpkin's bed (by this stage neither of us was using "Orpheus"). To settle him in, T. set up a small desk we'd originally bought secondhand for the tiny Balmain house.

She planned to work there for the first few evenings, until he got used to the room, felt it was his own, and wouldn't be afraid to be shut in for the night. She'd take her computer down, and whatever book she was reading, set them up on the desk beside the old bookshelf, now cluttered with boxes of potatoes and garlic heads, and he'd lie on the sofa, barely a meter away, watching her. Now and again I'd go down to say hello, or T. would come up to get something, but by and large they settled very quickly into a space entirely their own. The first few nights turned into a week, a fortnight, a month. It was often midnight, and sometimes much later, before she'd pack up her computer, top up his water bowl, feed him one last bottle, give him a handful of lucerne, and shut him in. It would be easy to characterize this as a maternal situation—and of course it was—but that seems hardly adequate. In truth this quiet, intimate space—the light filtering out through the latticed blind and part-opened door, onto the edge of the vegetable garden outside, the slowly turning pages, the raising and lowering of the lamb's head, their breathing, the movements of eyes, why each of them was there, what each felt about the other—was (as it still is) a deep thing, almost impossible to fathom.

I'd often be asleep by the time T. came up, and would almost always be awake before her. Before making coffee I'd prepare a bottle—he'd hear me from below and bleat in anticipation—and take it down to him, calling his name quietly as I did so. I'd push open the door and he'd be out, pushing at me, attacking the bottle with a thirst so great I'd have to brace myself so he didn't knock it out of my hand, or me to the ground.

It was early summer. He'd been castrated—in and out of the vets' within the day, with a full anesthetic and no visible side effects (but how could we tell?)—and the big boys had long been shorn (while he'd watched in lamb-like awe). The bushfire that, started by the military blunder, had devastated the 58,000 hectares of world heritage forest beside us, had miraculously not turned our way, the cicada season was over, the survivors of the September duckling tragedy had now learned to fly, and it was time for the next stage of Pumpkin's weaning.

Three or four meters to the east of the boys' coop was an old galvanized iron lean-to, two meters by one, open on the northern side, on a makeshift concrete slab. I boarded in the open side and made a little door—it felt like I was building at last the cubbyhouse I'd longed for in my early childhood (and tried to create out of old packing crates)—so that Pumpkin could have a room of his own, close enough to the boys to be able to hear them, but safe from foxes and any grumpy rumble that Henry or Jonathan might want to inflict. A few weeks here, we figured, might do it. We filled it with straw, put in a water bowl and a small box for his nighttime lucerne, and moved him in. T. had brought him down to visit several times as I'd constructed it, and again when she'd installed the hay, so that he was already familiar with the space, but closing him in, shutting the door, leaving him in the dark, would surely be another matter. On the first night we listened nervously for some anxious bleating, but there was nothing. Perhaps he was glad to be so near the others.

I would go down in the mornings to let him out and he'd attack the bottle with diminishing gusto. Somewhere in the third week, when I'd gotten up unusually early, I went down and found the little door mysteriously unhooked— who had done it? Jonathan? Henry? or had he rattled it free somehow?—and Pumpkin, un-rumbled, sitting in the coop with the others, contentedly chewing over his morning's grazing, just as they were.

All three of them looked at me as if they wondered why I'd come.

Orpheus sleeping

Six Rats and a Snake

In truth I've no idea how many rats there were. I've written "six" for the alliteration, so much of our Being being in this way a mirror-dance in the cage of our own mind. Our inner poetries determine more of our outer world than we think. That's one of the reasons why the occasional animals who visit that cage are so important. They have minds of their own, don't always follow the paths we think they will or that we want them to. Closely attended, they might offer us a way out, if we could ever free ourselves enough to follow them. I'd be pleasantly surprised if there *were* only six. But that, the not knowing, is a part of the story. The story? Well, no, not if you're expecting fiction, or even something with a clear beginning. Even my own beginning, here, is a bit arbitrary. My relationship with rats, not always something I'm proud of, goes way back.

For the time being we could say that it—this new part of the story—began when, in a new garden bed I'd prepared for the purpose out of the old, grass-covered ashpit on the sunny northern side of the cabin, I planted two rows of corn kernels, eight to a row.

Nine days later I was quietly pleased—it's always a special moment—to see three or four one-centimeter-high, deep-

135

green shoots, and think the first stage had succeeded. But then the next day, going down to see if there were more, I found only one shoot left, and nine neatly dug holes where other kernels had been. No trial and error. Every hole a bull's eye. A rat. Or rats. Surely. Who else could it have been? And I must say I was impressed at their keen sense of smell, to detect the kernels through two centimeters of soil. I'd tried to smell the kernels myself, dry and withered as they were, before I planted them. Nothing. But of course they'd had eight or nine days to soften. It was *germination* the rats had smelt. I was even more impressed. But also disappointed. More than half my crop, gone before it started.

I'd been stupid to plant it there in the first place, I suppose, right by the cabin. Why hadn't I *thought*? Gardening, growing, "farming," you have to calculate everything, be always a few steps ahead of where you think you need to be. Last year, before the writing room was built, Jonathan and Henry had got to my just-ripening tomatoes, demolished half the crop within two minutes when they'd breached my sheep-proof wire fence. I'd fixed the fence and watched the rest of the tomatoes ripen, or at least start to. And yet—a kind of optical illusion, it seemed at first, a literal now-you-see-it-now-you-don't—no sooner would I spy a tomato just turning the white-yellow that signals picking may be only a week away, than it would disappear. Birds? No. Some of these would-be tomatoes were far too big. A possum? Yes, quite possibly, come down from one of the towering eucalypts just over the fence. But then I noticed it happening from the tomato vines I'd planted in the raised bed in the old possum-proof chicken coop, in a part I'd fenced off so the sheep couldn't get to them. Unlikely a possum would get in there. Then it dawned on me: rats, coming out from the old farm shed or from under the cabin. Later confirmed by the tooth marks on the zucchinis in the same garden bed, fruit too large for the rats to actually pull off the plant and make away with. But for some reason the memory had not made its way into my plans for the new bed in the ashpit. I kicked myself. I hadn't even been prodded into more careful thought by the moment, two weeks before, when the rains came at last and, up at the house, I stood on the deck like the ancient mariner in the poem, looking at two furry rats scurry from the upper garden to shelter beneath the kitchen, blessing them unconsciously, as he'd blessed the water snakes.

War, I told myself, looking at the nine neat holes. This means war. I will out-*fox* them—a knowing metaphor, since I now live in a fox haunt. But not like the time, thirty years ago, when I killed thirty-one rats in the old poet's house, wrapped their bodies in newspaper, put them in the garbage, tried not to look into their shining, clear, penetrating eyes.

No, no killing: "humane" traps this time. It shouldn't be difficult. I'd bought one when we first moved in, and had since found another as I'd cleared the shed in readiness for its conversion. I had corncobs in the fridge. I'd cut the tips from those, use them as bait, and in the mornings—as many mornings as it took—I'd transport my captives, in the car, to some place out in the bush, too far away for them to be able to find their way back. I should catch the others under the house as well—they have a kind of highway in one of the walls, and make free with the roof space—before they chew through the wiring and the lights start to go out or we have a roof fire.

So I set a trap, the first. Carefully, in the midst of the previous night's rat excavations, wiping it free of any scent of me that might warn them off, and for good measure putting a few kernels into the holes they'd dug, filling them loosely, patting them down, so confident I was they'd not be able to resist the whole cob tip I'd put on the trip plate. But then— she does this over and again, gives voice to the thought I'm trying to suppress—T. said something, just as I was going to bed, about the poor creature who in the morning would be carried away from its habitat, its family. Already she'd made sure I put a small dish of water in the trap, mumbled about the sensitivity of rats, hoped that he or she wouldn't die of a heart attack before I could get there at first light—made me promise to carry the trap so carefully, with a sheet of stiff cardboard beneath the wire mesh base so that small rat feet wouldn't slip through the holes. I woke in the middle of the night and started thinking, trying without success to work out an alternative. The "humane" trap, at 2 a.m., didn't seem very humane at all.

But in the morning all was okay. The trap had shut, but no rat was inside, only the cob tip, tumbled from the trip plate. I felt disappointed and spared at the same time. How had they done it? The farm had been vacant, human-wise, for almost two years before we moved in. I could be pretty certain the rats wouldn't have seen such a trap before. So how could they know how to set it off without getting caught? Did they have a kind of folk memory, stories handed down from generation to generation? I had visions of one rat holding the trap door open while another went in and out, or of a particularly large, canny, athletic rat—and what rat isn't canny and athletic (Clumsy aside)?—holding the door open with his tail while grabbing the prize. But the prize was still there, and it needn't have happened that way anyway. The mechanism for setting the trap is (of course) *outside* the trap, and very sensitive. It would take only the slightest disturbance to set it off. Probably, in their nocturnal movements, a rat had tripped it without ever entering. That's why the cob tip was still there. To add insult to injury they'd dug up the last seven of the original, germinating kernels.

It all only hardened my resolve. I re-set the trap that evening, went down again next morning, car keys in pocket, ready for a relocation, guiltily conscious that I still hadn't decided where to take my captives. But it was the same as before, the trap set off, no rat. And again on the third morning, at which point, in frustration, turning my back on the whole matter, I left the trap there, door closed, cob tip tumbled on the mesh floor, like a forlorn monument to my folly, surrounded by small circular excavations that only now, writing this, I realize were like foxholes, left after a battle has been won.

Enter the snake, a few days later. But just *why* did she enter? What made her come? I sometimes think we're part of some drama being played out in us—"us" here referring to the whole panoply of creatures around us, the *herd* we human animals are part of without knowing it (this much the sheep have taught already)—of which we know only the tips, if we're conscious even of those. The previous night, T., who'd never, as far as she knows, dreamt of snakes before, had dreamt of a whole group of them in front of her on a path, and that one, a small one, had bit her finger. And only the weekend before, returning by train from the city, my mind had drifted— why?—to the killing of snakes and the way in my childhood, living in a town of dry-grassed backyards, snakes had made regular appearances. It had been almost a rite of passage, a test of courage, for Canberra husbands, or wives when the husbands couldn't face it, to kill snakes, usually by beheading them with a shovel. Probably, around suburban Australia, it's still the case. Depriving snake children of their mother or father. Killing whether the snake is a threat or not, whether it's trying to attack or only to escape. Killing because a snake tempted Eve. Killing because the Bible (or *The Jungle Book*, or *Indiana Jones and the Temple of Doom*) tells us how evil they are. Whereas my own sister, bitten so often and by such deadly specimens that she's lost a finger from necrosis and is no longer allowed to handle them because the antivenins will no longer work, has always loved them.

But I'm jumping the gun. All I'm really saying is that it seemed *foreshadowed* somehow, in a way I'd once have thought strange but have become so used to that it now seems more like the sporadic operation of a sense we don't know we have, let alone know what to do with. Across the front lawn, a two-meter Eastern Brown, moving rapidly toward the house, right between the hooves of Henry and Jonathan, who've raised their heads in mild surprise but don't seem particularly disturbed, as if, I thought only later, they knew the snake, had seen her before. At 4:40 p.m., after the first hot day in a while. On such days, when their blood has heated, snakes become active, and as the day's heat tails off—around 5 p.m., say—they'll get hungry, or need water. It may be that the snake knows about the old swimming pool, or that, hungry, she knows there are rats in the subfloor and is headed there. At two meters it's fair to assume she's a mature snake, perhaps five years old or older. And in all likelihood, since we're such new residents, she knows the place better than we. Like the rats, who probably have a sense of it we could never match. Nevertheless I have to fight off some crude, atavistic urge to head for a shovel. A killer rising in me—trained by my father's generation, as his had been by the one before it—along with alarm, a kind of panic, a brief eclipse of thought. Gone, thankfully, almost as quickly as she, but leaving me wondering, if only about how far there is yet to go, how many *obstacles in thought* there are before we begin to get things a little more right.

Did she get a rat? Perhaps. But if so it wasn't my ashpit visitor. Down there a few mornings later, checking on the bean plants that have at last come through—the rat doesn't seem interested in them—I notice that the excavations have continued. A hole has been dug *beneath* the trap, a tunnel, to enable him to get at the corncob tip that, when the trap closed for the last time, had tumbled into the center of the wire mesh floor, out of reach from either side. One can imagine this—the tumbled and ill-positioned corncob tip—to have been frustrating in the extreme, and the rat thinking about it when he woke in the midday, unable to get back to sleep, until that Eureka moment. Now, under there, he can reach up, mid-tunnel, and eat the corn at will, turn it whichever way he wants. Ingenious.

Rats, snake, let them go. With my secular blessing. My own Eureka moment. If you're afraid that the rats (or the rabbits, or the bowerbirds) will eat your vegetables, then grow more vegetables. Share.

Ethics, Etc.

Thought can't occur without language, they say—*I've* said—but I wonder. It seems to me a great deal of the world's thought occurs without anything we humans would recognize as language. I've been frustrated, lately, by not being able to find the time to get to my writing room and on with what I too often find myself thinking—a default position—is one of the main points of life. I'll think I see a clear space ahead but will then realize, say, as was the case a few days ago, that I haven't seen my neighbor Geoff around for days and that I should check on him (I haven't seen his sheep either, and his roosters have been strangely quiet) and, if I can find him, and he's all right, talk with him about some matters that have mounted up (the lower field, the fences, the council's attempt to prosecute him for letting his sheep range too freely); or I'll notice, at almost the same time I realize that, that there are rats in the peach tree, taking the last of the crop, and while I don't necessarily begrudge them—they're finding so much pleasure in it!—they did take a lot of tomatoes last year and, share as I'm happy to do, if we're to have a crop this time around then I should cage one of the tomato beds as soon as possible, having at last come to the realization (it's taken half a century) that when I work out something needs doing

I should do it immediately. Or, two days later, when, having spent more than I'd wanted of the previous day talking with Geoff (his wife's mother had died and he'd been lying low while his wife was away at the funeral; and yes, he's defeated the council in court, but conceded a provision that he fence off a small stand of protected trees on our land—he said he'd do this a year ago—before letting his flock graze there again ... etc., etc.), I'm fencing off a tomato bed and find that Orpheus, who so far has nibbled only at the edges of the potato plants, has developed a taste for them (and corn shoots, and lettuce). While I don't begrudge him a few leaves, he has no sense of sharing and so I have to make other arrangements about this also.

Fair enough. These, and dozens of other tasks like them, are small things, and needn't prevent writing, but they do take time and energy, and when, one or another of them done, a piece of time does appear, as often as not—*more* often than not—the mood to write, that delicate balance of inner and outer factors, has passed. All a matter of prioritizing, you might think, but for some reason I've rarely if ever given the writing the priority over the demands of the immediate, and it is this reason that I want, here, to think (write) about.

I've always believed that writing must work its way through the demands of everyday necessity; that it gains strength from this and is weaker without it. I still believe this, though I'd now phrase it differently. What I'd now say, to my frustrated self, without for a moment denying that frustration is part of the process, is that writing *is already going on* in and through such things; that they *are already* a form of writing. There's a *thinking* that goes on as one plans a wire coop, or cage (call it *coop*, I like that), for one's tomato plants, searches under the house—watching for the snake—for mesh tight enough to prevent rats passing through, measures and cuts that mesh, places it panel by panel on the four sides of the tomato bed, carefully holding back the tomato vines so as not to break off any of the early fruit, wires the corners together, cuts back an overhanging peach-tree branch which rats—so smart they are!—might use as a springboard into the tomatoes, etc. A thinking most of which is before words, although here and there it erupts into them, or *they* erupt. A thinking—since it involves the hands so much, and the sense of balance as one steps over garden borders, treads carefully so as not to injure eggplant seedlings or garlic stems—that's every bit as much a matter of the body as it is of the mind. These are activities on the borders of one's being (what activities are not?), drawing (if you like, or if you must) *Being* into *that* being, *World* into one's own world, *Other* into self, or vice versa. And, of course, drawing them towards language. And, I'd also say, these things are *ethical*—or, rather, that the *process* is an ethical one, since it ties these things together, connects tomato to fence, rat to peach tree, ethics to garlic stems, potato beds to writing, and insists that they work it out, that they all get along.

❧

The first recorded use in English of the word "ethology," according to the *Oxford English Dictionary*, is in the *Glossographia* (lovely word) of Thomas Blount in 1656, in which it's defined as "the feat of counterfeiting mens manners, an interlude of a moral subject, or wherein mens manners are acted and expressed." More recently it's come to mean the study of (non-human) animal behavior. Obviously there's been a shift, but one can see the connection. The *OED* traces the word back to the Greek, connects it with *ethos*, and so with *ethics*.

The second meaning the *OED* gives for "ethology," along with an earliest citation from 1678 (E. Phillips's *New World of Words*) and the notation *obs* ("obsolete"), is "The science of ethics; also, a treatise on manners or morals," thus, at one touch, making my point for me: that ethics are intricately involved in our studies of human and other animal behavior, and that, further and more importantly, ethics can and should be seen as species specific, in a way that should prepare us for the difficulties we encounter when, as oftentimes we must, we try to apply *human* ethics to guide us in our relations with one or another *non*-human species.

To work in a broader, more flexible ethical field. It's not an immensely difficult proposition—though I'd be the last to claim I've successfully done so—but it does require caution, openness, a readiness to see one's assumptions, the things one thinks one *knows*, overturned. After all, *non*-human animals do it far more often than we. Throw a ball to a dog and he'll likely chase it, as he'll do any fast-moving creature (a ball, a rat, a rabbit, a postman, a car), because he's of a *predator* species. Throw a ball to a sheep and she's more likely to back away, being instinctively predisposed, as a *prey* species, to beware fast-moving creatures. A dog and a lamb might wish to play with one another, but they'll have some sorting out to do. Each will, in effect, extend their front limbs and lower their heads—the invitation to the game, or the bow before it begins—but whereas it's the dog's predisposition to bark, it's the lamb's to butt. Eventually they may compromise; *chasings* might even be possible, provided it's not the dog's intention to catch and devour. These simple behaviors are a gesture only, toward a skein of behaviors and encroachments and respects that it would serve us, and *our* herd, to wake up to.

led, through that crack, by a dog, a few sheep, some ducks, a rat

A Drizzly Day

A drizzly day, and cooler, after heat. The sheep are invigorated. Henry is up on the cabin deck, wanting someone to play with him. No one is there. Eventually he comes down and charges across the paddock to the wild ducks. Used to his antics, they simply part as he approaches and let him barge through.

Attempts at contact. This morning two unripe cherry tomatoes, in their usual place on the kitchen floor. If I leave them to ripen on the vine, chances are the rats will get them before I do, so for a while now I've picked them just as they begin to lighten, and brought them inside to ripen in the morning sun on the windowsill. But now my indoor rat—or mouse, I still don't know which—has found them, and every morning for the last week or so has left me two of the ripest, nibbled to various extents, at almost exactly the same place on the carpet runner at the foot of the plate cupboard. As often as not there'll be a third, half-eaten rather than nibbled, somewhere in the living room. Evidently he/she (let's say "he") has some way of getting up onto the kitchen bench, and then onto the windowsill. Does he then carry the tomatoes down, or drop them and go down afterward? I know that when *I* drop one on the carpet it rolls: there's no way I could get it to stop every time in the same place. So I imagine, unless he suffers from a kind of obsessive compulsive disorder and *must* return each rolled tomato to the same spot, he *carries* them down. But why put them, every time, in exactly the same place?

For a little while I think I stymied him—I now place all the *ripe* tomatoes in a large porcelain bowl which, every evening, I cover with a colander, leaving the unripe ones to their fate—but there again this morning, two unripe tomatoes from the windowsill (but the ripest of the un-ripe), in the usual place below. I picked them up, finding them almost completely unmarked, and then, three meters away, about to sit down to the computer to check the news, a third, half-eaten, at my feet.

For the life of me I can't work out why he doesn't ever fully eat the first, or go back for the second and third. They're like a message. I don't know what it says, but perhaps that doesn't matter. Perhaps it's just *phatic*, as Malinowski would say.[39] *I'm here. Don't imagine I'm not.*

39 Bronisław Malinowski, "The Problem of Meaning in Primitive Languages," in C.K. Ogden and I.A. Richards, *The Meaning of Meaning* (1923), ninth edition (New York and London, 1953).

Mushroom Season

March already. We've had a lot of rain lately, after the long dry summer; warm temperatures interspersed with the first chills of autumn. The garden, after giving us a glut of them, has produced one last round zucchini; the Lebanese eggplants, which I'd never expected to grow at all, are clustered and heavy on their stems; the last of a large crop of tomatoes is ripening rapidly amongst dying leaves; the sheep, I suspect it's Jonathan, have broken into the ashpit garden and eaten all the bean plants—and there seem to be fungi almost everywhere I look.

A week ago the front lawn was carpeted with thousands of tiny red caps, and on an old stump hard by the north fence was a bouquet of wood fungus so perfectly scalloped, of such a creamy yellow in the half-light, that for a moment it had me forgetting to breathe. Amongst the eggplants were several ragged-edged, asymmetrical white toadstools, at the center of each a perfect five-pointed star, though not so much a marking on the skin as a healed cut, a wound, and in the half darkness among the tomato vines, in a small, covered clearing where the rats have left a carnage of half-eaten fruit, a stand of three mushrooms of the deep burnt orange that I think is called alizarin red, glistening, almost as if some creature had just been sacrificed there. All of them gone now, withered and dry, though a few days ago I watched a black mushroom breaking through, a dark muscular bloom, hefting a small clod on its shoulders, like a miniature Henry Moore sculpture, a tiny Atlas. I was in a rush and so did not stop, and when I looked the next day couldn't find it. Then yesterday, in a different part of the yard, there were two fist-sized mushrooms—mushrooms? toadstools? who's to tell?—of a deep, leathery brown, gnarled and ancient-looking, that I think must be of the same variety, and today there are dozens, that will themselves be shrunken and dry in a few days' time.

The lawn that's producing all these wonders is also full of holes. From this year's cicadas, from funnel-web spiders (curtained, theirs are, just inside the entrance, with a fine muslin, a coin of mist), or the dung beetles that have just begun to colonize, thriving on the sheep droppings. Ants, I thought they were initially, making these small pyramids of fine-crumbled soil—soil *meal*—and wondered where they had come from so suddenly, but no, dung beetles, breaking down the sheep- and duck-droppings, and probably Charlie's also. Ashes to ashes, dust to dust, soil to soil.

I will have to be careful with the drenching. Poison given to the sheep to kill the parasites they pick up from their constant ground- and dropping-level grazing will become poisonous dung, killing the very beetles that are taking it away. But—I've just been checking—there are alternatives. Cider vinegar, with wormwood (so that's where it got its name! a *vermifuge*, or *anthelmintic*), nasturtium, tansy, pumpkin seeds, or a simpler concoction of vinegar, garlic, and molasses. There had to be ways before the big stock companies got into the game. Ancient ways. So much to learn. We were growing wormwood at the previous house, though more out of respect for the *symboliste* poets and my daughter's sudden interest in absinthe (wormwood's botanical name is Artemisia

Absinthium) than for medicinal reasons. But now …

I'm pretty sure it was only grain Henry was expelling when he vomited yesterday. He stopped suddenly, then began to walk slowly forward with his head down, twisting it to the side in a way that seemed to indicate he had something stuck in his throat. Then, increasingly agitated, he jumped, all four feet off the ground, just as he does in the middle of play (astonishing, the strength in a sheep's legs), though clearly this was no game. Then expelled—projected—a meter-long string of yellowish mucus, laden with the grains T. had just fed him, to lure him back inside the front gate through which he'd strayed when she was taking out the car. Seeds going down the wrong way, I thought, but it's rare for a sheep to vomit—in fact quite difficult, given their complicated stomach—and usually a sign that something is seriously wrong.

T. went in to the computer and within minutes came back with a likely diagnosis of fungal poisoning, which apparently can neutralize the bacteria in a sheep's stomach so the sheep can't digest any more, vomits his food instead, and eventually starves to death (no cure apparently, though a woman in Britain has been reintroducing bacteria into her ewe's stomach with a preparation of herbs and yogurt). We watched Henry closely and T. checked the paddock for any other vomit, but there was nothing and he's kept all his food down since, so with luck he's okay, but for a while there I was seeing all these wonderful mushrooms from a different perspective.

There's not much reliable lore about Australian mushrooms, at least not at large amongst the invader population. It seems even indigenous Australians are divided. Some use them for food and medicines; others avoid them entirely. Last year a recent Chinese immigrant saw familiar-looking mushrooms in a pine forest near Canberra and made a meal of them for a friend. Within two days both men were dead from massive organ failure. Death caps. I see that this year the A.C.T. government has issued a warning. Fourteen fatalities in the last five years from death caps, the article said, which makes them statistically far more lethal than the funnel-web or any other of the deadly non-mushroom creatures on this tiny farm (by which I'm thinking mainly of the snake, whom we've begun to call Sybil, as much for the *sibilance* as for any oracular powers she might have).

There are seasons of thought, too. Information comes in mushroom-like clusters. Last week we re-housed one of Geoff's sheep. We'd had such success finding a home for Molly the goat that he thought of us for a ewe whose latest lamb had been stillborn, and whom he didn't think should get pregnant again. Kind of him from one perspective, I guess, to think of her retirement—she'd already had a number of lambs by the sound of it, five in the last year, he said (!)—though it's as likely he doesn't want to waste his time and pasturage (some of it ours) on a ewe whose lambs aren't going to make it, or whom he has to segregate from rams.

T. went to see her and then quizzed Geoff further. It turns out he'd thought the lamb might have died because she, the ewe, had pulpy kidney. He'd vaccinated her, he said, and she should be fine now, but perhaps—and saying nothing about his odd understanding of vaccination—that explains why he hadn't taken the other and (for him) even more obvious route of killing and eating her. A superstition about diseased flesh, or flesh that's just been injected with a powerful vaccine. Whatever. We were being given a chance to save her, so we asked no more questions. An argument or whiff of disapproval and we might not be given the opportunity next time.

Still, pulpy kidney didn't sound too good, so we arranged to take her to Mark for a check. We'd have to do this anyway if we were going to try to re-home her. Geoff met us there, with the ewe, whom T. had already decided to call "Princess" (Geoff never names his sheep), and Mark examined her. Geoff mentioned pulpy kidney again, and that he'd vaccinated her; in the ensuing conversation it became clear this was the first time he'd ever done so. Mark's disapproval was evident.

I asked about pulpy kidney. Are *our* sheep at risk? Should *we* vaccinate? All the principal diseases of sheep, Mark explained, have the same basic cause, a dramatic increase in one or another of the populations of bacteria already present in the gut, an increase that can come from a sudden excess or a change of feed, from grass to grain, for example. I nodded as if I knew this already, committing every word to memory. But clearly Princess was okay. No pulpy kidney. A bit of arthritis in her legs, not uncommon for her age, and hooves needing trimming—another tacit reprimand to Geoff.

T. drew up a description and a brief biography and put out a call for help. Molly, six months before, had received numerous offers, became almost an instant celebrity, but for Princess there was almost nothing. This may have been because we'd said she'd been part of a herd and mightn't thrive alone, and at the same time that it would not be good for her to be exposed to a ram, but it might also have been because she was more clearly a farm animal, whereas Molly had been a pet. Then we remembered Mary and Billie, whom we'd deprived of boyfriends eighteen months before, and whom we'd come to think of as the Lonely Ewes. There may not have been grass enough for four, but perhaps a third wouldn't stretch them too far. We called, and the case was suddenly easy: Don and Sue were not only willing but were excited at the prospect.

We went to pick her up two days later. I'm unsteady on my feet and so left it to T. to help Geoff yard her, trim her hooves, and load her into the van. While they were trying to coax her—she seemed to sense something major was happening and was quite reluctant—I watched the other ewes through the gate, struck as always by the particular soft beauty of this breed (they are Dorpers, a kind that sheds its own wool, doesn't need shearing) but also by the sadness of seeing them without the lambs that just weeks before would meet me by our bottom fence. Geoff says he sells his lambs only for breeding, but I know many of them end up on carving plates. There was probably a lot of grief in the wan stares these ewes were giving me on this overcast morning. One of them, surely, would have been Princess's best friend; perhaps some were her sisters or daughters. Grief upon grief.

Geoff cut one of Princess's hooves too closely. She was bleeding as she was lifted into the van. Probably she hated us all, that trip, and I'm glad it was only twenty kilometers. T. and I both wished we could explain to her what was happening, that this was to save her life. But there's no explaining. There was one bleat, as she found her van-legs, then silence, apart from the roar of the engine. At Sue and Don's she would not get out at first, but then suddenly leapt and made a run for it, tearing the lead from T.'s hand. Luckily the only clear path was down into the paddock where Mary and Billie, the Lonely Ewes, were waiting. By the time the rest of us got there she was already making their acquaintance. She still had the lead on, however, and that was a problem. There's scrub up the back. If the lead got caught on something she could strangle herself. T. and Don followed her about for an hour, all over the paddock and up into the forest, but she wouldn't let them near. Eventually Don came back, bushed, but T. kept at it and about ten minutes later Princess returned, with T. several meters behind her, to all appearances shepherding her without her knowing it, though I think it's just as likely Princess had checked out the place and decided to come back of her own volition. Keeping an eye on us, as if daring us to try to get the lead again, she began to graze near her new companions. At least I hope that's what they are by now. We left, T. and I, on the too-many-cooks principle; Don could drop the lead in next time he came up the mountain. At seven-thirty that night, four hours later, there was a message: "Cindy"—they'd named her after Cindy Lauper (Lauper/Dorper) – "is unshackled and hanging with the ewes. Retirement plan back on track."

Apparently sheep can remember a lot of faces, and for a long time. A herd thing, I guess, and though they're sheep faces, not human ones, I wonder, if we ever see her again, whether Cindy will remember us—the odds sound good that she would—and, if she does, whether it will be as those horrid beings who took her from her herd, wounded her foot, shoved her into the darkness of a van, and chased her around in the scrub for an hour, or whether she might have come to the idea instead that we're the people who brought her to a home she's come to love or at least feel safe in, with no rams bothering her and no one taking her children away. It's a tough call, but I hope it's the latter, if only because I think it's the attitude that might bring her the greater peace of mind. We all need that.

They say mushrooms can be huge plants, and that what we see are only the blooms. I don't know if that's right—though I guess it might explain some of the patterns they make in our own lawn (their circles, their lines ...)—but when I heard this I envisioned a tree underground, a tree we wouldn't know how to recognize if we dug for it, a tree we'd need a different sense to see. This afternoon, crossing a part of the lawn I hadn't been to for a day or two, I found, in a kind of arc, twenty or thirty large white mushrooms that hadn't been there last time I looked. I wonder if I can *plant* myself at last, Antaeus-like, and what roots I can send down, into all this. Loose the thought from its aerial keep, its dangerous castle.

I can't remember if there were mushrooms this time last year. I suppose there were, and that it's just a matter of my inattention, but perhaps mushroom season, like cicada season, isn't an annual event. It's been quite a year. Henry's castration, Bobbi's death, the cicadas, the duckling tragedy, the attack on

Charlie, the coming of Pumpkin, so feeble at first but already so robust and independent he's not only been accepted by the others but sometimes seems to be leading them. You'd think we might rest a while, catch our breath, but I suspect that's not ever going to be the way. I've at last found a fencer who'll take on the swamp, though we'll have to wait until summer when the water level's low. Once we've a fence there we can safely let the boys down to get to the rich grass on the other side— breathing space for the upper paddock—but it'll also mean protecting the swamp ecology somehow. T.'s already talking about someday repairing the old railway-sleeper causeway, and her somedays are never far away. Beyond the fences, over the bridges, there's such a vastness of animal suffering you don't know where to start, only that you have to. I thought I might be able to keep it at bay, just for this book, but I suspect all this could ever be is a glimpse, a threshold.

Kicking Rilke

Charlie's early morning habits are a study. I've sometimes wished I knew less about them. Although I tend to go to bed well after midnight I don't often sleep more than five or six hours. It's never been quite enough for me. It's not his paddings about that wake me, but they certainly don't help return me to sleep.

If I wake particularly early—at three or four, for example— I've a better chance of dropping off again, particularly if I can keep myself from thinking about the work I'm doing. At such hours I may find myself, as I lie in the dark, trying to tell the sound of the frogs from the sound of the crickets, or counting (counting, a neurosis of mine) the components of the songs of one or the other. The tree frogs in this area chirp most often nine times in rapid succession, but will sometimes stretch to eleven or even thirteen (such a fondness for uneven numbers!). Or I'll count the crowing of the roosters: two at Geoff's place (one loud and deep-throated, the second thinner, more raspy), a third softer and farther off, and a fourth, even farther away, whom I hear only on still nights or if a breeze is blowing in the right direction. I count, at the same time, the seconds, in my head, and the number of cock crows on my fingers—a challenging task when, as they will in the hour before dawn, they crow, all together, as often as ten or fifteen times per minute (imagine: six to nine hundred times per hour!). The phrase from the Bible concerning Peter's betrayal of Christ "before the cock crows thrice" around here would mean "in a matter of seconds."

Geoff used to have three roosters. The deep-throated one, the raspy one (who never seems to be able to complete his crow), and a third whose crow—it had the classic shape we are taught in preschool, *cock-a-doodle-doooo*—I'd wait for, proud and pure, my favorite. One particularly loud night—there must have been a fox in the area and the roosters were sending out warnings—I heard him taken, mid-call. His crow turned to a horrid shriek which was choked off almost instantly. Ever since then there's been a kind of lameness to the ritual, a voice missing.

And then of course there's the morning chorus itself. I'll lie there as the light begins to creep through the venetians, trying to identify the different birds, the finches from the mynahs (not easy, since mynahs mimic so many others), the mynahs from the mountain lowries, the lowries from the butcherbirds and bowers, thrilling, as I still do, to the whipbirds and the way they cut through it all.

But I was writing about Charlie. He'll wake, most mornings, around six and go out for a pee. His regular breathing (what does he dream about?) will change and I'll hear a stirring from the beanbag beside the bed, the sound of his stretching, then the tap of his claws on the floorboards as he makes his way to the dog door in the pantry. I'll hear the dog door swing as he goes out, then again as he re-enters. He'll then roll around on his back on the living room rug for a while before taking a drink from his bowl (an iambic meter, his lapping there), then coming back into the bedroom and onto the beanbag to wash himself. Some nights he has trouble sleeping. I'll hear him pad from room to room, looking for the most comfortable place to settle, or go in and out of the dog door as if the moon is making him restless or he thinks there's a fox about. If any morning I choose to get up before he's gone soundly back to sleep he'll come over to me and begin to lick my feet, my lower legs, my knees, as much as possible before I manage to clothe myself, as if the taste of my skin were one of the most delicious he's encountered. I can't imagine that it is and wonder what Carol the dog trainer would say about it. Charlie licks Henry's or Jonathan's ears and face when he's in the mood and either of them is inclined to let him, a tender spectacle that can go on for ten minutes or so, but is also as likely as not to lick his beanbag or his blanket on the couch, as if they were extensions of himself. Carol would probably say it's a dominance/submission thing, but I think it's just affection. I can't see why any dog would need to dominate or be submissive to his beanbag.

It's interesting how writing can lead you. When I sat down today I hadn't thought of saying any of this—the roosters, the morning chorus, Charlie's licking in the half dark. I was going instead to write about his new habit. But perhaps you need to know about the nights as well as the days; what we can know of them, anyway: what Charlie hears as he lies there; what the boys listen to when they lie in the coop or graze out in the never-but-almost dark (what did *they* think, when they heard the rooster die?). Not that there aren't bleats out there, too, especially when there are lambs about, but for the most part the sheep pass their nights in silence.

A few months ago, preparing to write a long-planned essay, I was re-reading the great Czech/German poet Rilke. One night I took the book to bed with me and, after a few pages, now tired enough to sleep, put it, open at the page I'd come to, facedown beside the bed (a bad habit, I'm told, cluttering the floor in this way: Rilke wasn't alone down there), and the next night, and the next, had other things to read. It must have been a week before I looked for Rilke again. Not finding him by the bed, I looked elsewhere through the house and cabin but without success. I was puzzled but went on to the next task and put the missing book out of my mind. We then went away for a week, and my sister came up to look after the house and Charlie and the sheep. When I got back, to my surprise, the Rilke was on my bedside table.

"Where did you find it?" I asked.

"Under the bed," she said. "I thought I'd vacuum and there it was."

Under the bed? A mystery. But now that I had it back I could return to my essay. The process, however, repeated itself. I read some poems before going to sleep and, when ready to turn out the light, put the book down beside the bed. It was a restless night. At about four, half awake, I heard a scrabbling beside me. I didn't want to turn on the light to see what was happening—it was clearly Charlie—and the light would only disturb T. and make it harder for me to go back to sleep. I stuck my hand out, found Charlie's back, scratched it, got a lick for my trouble, and rolled over.

By the next morning I'd forgotten all about it. Two nights later, however, when I wanted the Rilke again, it wasn't there. I remembered where my sister said she'd found it and, sure enough, there it was, far under the bed. Puzzled—it was taking a long time to click—I picked it up, read awhile, then once more put it on the floor beside the bed. This night—or earliest morning, I should say—I was lying there thinking, the first light creeping into the room, when I heard Charlie's scrabbling again. I rolled over quietly and watched as, inch by inch, he nosed/pawed/kicked the Rilke under the bed. When presumably he'd got it far enough out of sight he turned to come out and—I could hear this distinctly—gave it one last shove with his hind leg before emerging.

Why? More to the point, why Rilke? There'd been other

books down there over the last month or so, some lighter, some heavier, some smaller, some larger, but they'd stayed more or less where they were. This seemed almost personal. Rilke's long been a favorite of mine. I number his elegies amongst the great poems of the last century. But how could Charlie know that? And in some ways Rilke's a pioneer as an *animal* poet. Animals, he says (meaning non-human ones), live wholly within the moment, whereas humans have lost this capacity. *Our* present is always contaminated by our preoccupation with the past and our hopes or anxieties about the future. Our sense of time has divorced us from our *being-as-it-happens*, and so has language, which filters the world about us, determining how we see, and even what we're able to see in the first place. Words become substitutes for the things they represent, depriving those things of much of their intensity and presence. We've isolated ourselves in our *interpreted* world, Rilke says, put ourselves into a kind of cage. Animals, on the other hand, live in what he calls the *Open*.

Even more alluring is the way he uses his own poetry—the way he treats things and the moment *in* that poetry—as a means of showing us how we might stick our heads out of the cage and breathe a bit of the Open for ourselves. His poems, at their best, try to give back to things some of the intensity, mystery, and weight of existence that the distracted human mind has come to overlook. Don't try to impress the angels with your speculations about metaphysical things, he says, they know far more about them than you ever will; tell them about *this* world.

What he has to say about animals can still seem almost revolutionary. Look at most human artifacts, and animals, if they're there at all, are little more than decoration, accessory. Rilke's one of the first poets I know to place human and non-human animals in an almost equal spiritual relation, or to say with any kind of intellectual conviction that non-human animals have ways of being from which we could learn and so, perhaps, start to heal an ancient wound.

But there are also things in Rilke's statements about animals that are contradictory and perplexing. I first got the idea of writing my essay when I came across, in this poet who wrote so significantly and suggestively about animals, a couple of poems that actually condone hunting.[40] His talk about addressing angels, too, bothers me. To pay attention to a metaphysical realm at all, it seems to me, is to reduce our attention and sensitivity to this one. And to say that language is the barrier seems to discount the possibility—the *reality*—that non-human animals have their own languages, and so might live in their *own* interpreted worlds. We're all in this together. As to that enticing idea that animals *live in the moment*, undistracted by thought of past and future, well, like so many other things, that says far more about human than non-human animals. How would we know? I've a strong suspicion that, when Jonathan sits gazing into the distance, oblivious to my greeting, he's remembering some thing or another.

I doubt, however, that any of these things were in Charlie's mind as he kicked Rilke under the bed. Why he should have singled out Rilke is still a mystery, but, as I've said before, he has a good nose. He reads a patch of clover or tussock of spear grass—or, in the park, a rain-soaked tissue or morsel of excrement—like a scholar. Perhaps he caught a whiff of insincerity or error. It seems to me you're never so aware of the rubbish you're harboring than when you speak it into the face or place it under the nose of an animal. Even if it was only that, sensing I might be waking, he wanted to come over to stand beside me, and was annoyed to find a book in the way, isn't that, at one remove, almost the same?

40   See my finished essay, "At Duino," in *Derrida's Breakfast* (Blackheath: Brandl & Schlesinger, 2016).

A month has gone by, anyway, and I've finished my essay. Rilke's no longer beside the bed. Like so many others, now I've made this "animal turn," I doubt I'll read him again with quite the same pleasure. A generous friend recently gave me a beautiful edition of a work I've long been curious about, a set of letters written by a Mr. Gilbert White of Hampshire to some naturalist friends in the 1760s and '70s and published in 1789, the year after the first fleet arrived in Australia. *The Natural History of Selborne.* My heart sank when, only a few pages in, charmed already, I realized that, when White was curious about one or another of the birds he describes so lovingly in the woods about him, he'd have someone go out and shoot it so that he could take a closer look. That's just not on.

Imagine my feelings, then (surprise? delight? confirmation?), when, getting up this morning, I found that Charlie had kicked this, too—a heavy hardback, with marbled cover, quite unlike the light, white Rilke—far into the darkness under the bed.

Good Friday

Good Friday. Bright sunshine. Quiet. One of those mornings to handle like a brimming cup. There was once a hushed holiness to this day but now it's a hush of a different kind, as if predators were about and one daren't make a sound for fear of attracting them. One *can* have quiet, yes—I'm having it now—and with shops closed and so many people on the highways heading for long-weekend destinations, and others observing the rituals or thinking that *you* are, the usual static of phone calls, e-mails, shopping, and appointments is at a minimum, but one carries the cup all the more carefully, as if the ground were mined, or its dust laced with toxins one dare not disturb.

There *are* toxins in the rituals; the ceremonies are no longer innocent. They never were, but now we see it. T. is nervous about leaving this place tomorrow, as we're committed to do, for fear someone will steal Pumpkin for their Easter lamb. Up and down the streets are rabbit cages, six or seven we've seen so far, as if (for it's as much a time of rabbit as lamb) one must display one's victim before eating him. But perhaps I get that wrong: the intention may simply be to have an Easter rabbit for a pet, rather than to slaughter and devour (for who around here nowadays, apart from Geoff, or Randall down the road, kills and prepares their meat themselves?). Maybe it's more the display of a prisoner. A pet, or symbol, or both (people seem to have developed the bad habit of giving others rabbits as Easter gifts; most of them end up in pounds or released into the wild). Yet the slaughter and devouring are real enough. One eats fish on Good Friday—a personal "sacrifice," abstaining from meat to mark the sacrifice of Christ—and on Easter Sunday eats lamb, again a practice laden with religious symbolism, supposedly underlain by a pagan vegetation rite. Easter is early spring in the northern hemisphere; I imagine the first lambs coming onto the market. I can't look at butchers' displays anymore, but from memory they're full at this time with the carcasses of rabbits and the thighs of lambs, many of the latter quite large since spring in the southern hemisphere came six months earlier. Pumpkin is almost seven months already.

And Jonathan has hurt himself. Come a cropper somehow. Yesterday afternoon I went down to the cabin and he was on the deck waiting. Obliquely, as he does, not like Henry who'll come directly up. I noticed there was a string of saliva coming from his mouth. Looking more closely I saw a pink patch, like a wound, on his left cheek, that hadn't been there an hour before. The cheek looked swollen. I came back to the house and Googled "sheep" and "drool" together but got nothing. No horrid sudden disease. No. A wound. Spiked himself on a tree branch, probably, or walked into a stick while grazing. I went back and looked again. He wouldn't let me examine it too closely, but as I rubbed his ear and murmured some sympathy he peed, a sign of pleasure normally, or maybe in this case relief, as if I'd done something right and he'd got something he needed. Recognition of his hurt.

We're off for a break, to stay a couple of days down on the coast with Philip (a philosopher) and Alice (a linguist)—vegans and "animal people"—and to meet their rescued guinea pigs and alpacas. My sister's come from Lithgow again to look after

Charlie and the boys. There's a chill in the air but it's a morning of margarine sun. As we're about to head for the car, the young black dog we found on the road and, to keep her safe from the traffic, took to the RSPCA last weekend—nowhere else at that hour to take her—is back again, as she's been almost every day since, wearing a red collar now, sniffing at the gate. It's not clear which side of the gate is prison, that side or this, or whether, since it's all a vast prison as far as most animals are concerned, the gate and the fence merely separate one prison section from the next. Or whether they are right or wrong, this dog's human companions, to let her roam so "free." Certainly she seems happy enough, but it's only a matter of time before she's hit by a car or one of the huge trucks that barrel past every hour or so from the council depot.

When we arrive Philip has a migraine, has taken one of his famous pills, and is sleeping deeply. Alice introduces us to the guinea pigs, in a room of their own, surrounded by a fifteen-centimeter-high bamboo fence that reminds me immediately of the barricade on Axel's island in Joseph Conrad's *Victory*, or perhaps of an Amazonian village. A token barricade— they could scramble over it if they wished—but they seem to appreciate it, and behind it huts and a meeting hall made of cardboard boxes with doors and windows cut into them; a hay basket and a small pedestal dining table for feeding. Heidi, Jess, and Sally (the eldest, with a golden coat). An hour and a half here, meeting them and having some lunch outside, before driving an hour south to the property of another friend, Melinda, where the alpacas are staying, in a lush paddock with an elderly cow and her daughter, surrounded by other paddocks in which there are more cows and steers, all rescued from the industrial process. Thick green grass in golden afternoon light.

As the ground is a bit too uneven for me I stay with the alpacas, Otto and Xeny, initially photographing T. while she meets them, and then handing the camera to her, to take down to meet the cows, while Alice goes to the barn for hay. They say alpacas are good with sheep, that they'll defend a flock ferociously against wild dogs and other predators. But they're such strange, beautiful creatures it's hard to imagine any ferocity in them. Their eyes so large and the rims so dark you'd think they'd been made up with kohl: a permanent look of surprise, though that cannot be. In the near dusk, as the sunshine leaves the field, I seem to hear them talking to one another.

When T. and Alice come back up we go to an adjoining paddock to meet the steers—in fact four steers and, now, a young black cow who recently broke into this paddock for a third time, whether for company or having heard it's a place of refuge isn't clear. On the first two occasions Melinda returned her, but now it's happened again she's letting her stay. I'm enthralled by the stunning coat of the steer they call Milo— just that color, but shimmering, almost opalescent. So huge, so strong, so sleek, a young god. I can't take my eyes from him.

A *compound experience*, you'd have to say—such peace with the animals, and such wonder, but all the while something else in the air, a scent—stink—of an Easter barbeque. The tenants on the neighboring property, less than fifty meters away, have been having a long lunch al fresco with friends. It's an occasion, by the looks of it, of a kind I might once have enjoyed. I could be looking at my earlier self, and a current of shame runs through me. How could the peace of these animals be a true peace (do I see it, that peace? or only, like Rilke, presume?) when, in the air around them, there hangs the smell of the cooked flesh of others? I can accept that the alpacas seem glad to see Alice—clearly they are!—and that the cows and steers are glad to be given hay, but surely the mere presence of humans, ourselves included, must put them on edge.

As we are meeting the steers—the new cow standing

nervously in the background, Milo's coat opalescent in the waning light—three of these neighbors, who've been walking twenty minutes now out in the paddocks, pass close by. They seem to feel they should speak with us. Neighborly curiosity. Nice people, I guess—academics from the nearby university—but also, one senses, vaguely bemused by these "animal people" who keep alpacas, cows, geese *to no purpose.* Alice speaks with them across the fence. T. and I hang back—a bit like the new cow herself. A combination of not knowing what to say, and biting our tongues. It's hard not to see such people as of the vast majority to whom a revelation has not yet come, beings mired in cruelty whether they realize it or not; and on their part they probably see people like us (me), in one of those ancient instilled binaries—fences—we just have to forget about, as *weak, debased* somehow, self-*demeaned* (an interesting term there: demeaned = de-meaned = taken from the *mean,* but also departing from *meaning*), not to mention *sanctimonious, self-righteous,* etc. I, too, probably, would once have smiled condescendingly at what I've now become. But there's no going back, nor any shred of wanting to.

Home to Philip then, another hour's drive through the autumn dusk and into the early night. And, finding him still sleeping, a simple dinner and some wine, a while playing with the guinea pigs on the couch, and later, when Alice asks what I'm writing and I tell her about Charlie and the dusk, an account, from her, of alpacas and *their* dusk anxiety. "Did you hear them," she asks, "as I was talking to those people at the fence? In the background? That sound Otto and Xeny made? Their *creaky* voice? Alpacas stand together at dusk every evening, and look around them, making that sound. As dark gets closer they become concerned about predators. At night, when they sleep, they take it in turns to keep watch. Otto and Xeny do it even now. Ancient conditioning. Fear of the cougar and the jaguar."

I guess dusk anxiety can take many forms. As can the cougar and the jaguar. The next morning Philip is up before us, his migraine gone. We talk over breakfast about the Theory of Non-Existent objects, one of our mutual entertainments, and about how Australian philosophy has had a strange strength in alternative theories of logic. We sit outside, watching the guinea pigs play in their newly constructed outdoor range, and Philip cooks us vegan pizzas. Then, late already, we hit the road. It's Easter Saturday, and we've a dinner appointment in Canberra to talk with a couple, Collette and Jim, about their planned protests against this year's monstrous kangaroo cull.

The highway is dotted with corpses, as usual, most of them thankfully dragged to the verge by council workers or Good Samaritan drivers. Or perhaps the creatures have managed to drag themselves there, with their last strength before dying. Kangaroos, wallabies, wombats, foxes, or birds that have become so glutted feeding on them they haven't been able to lift themselves out of the traffic. It's soon dusk. Although we're at risk of being late, we slow to well below the speed limit, since dusk is the time when most of these animals are hit. We should stop, at least for the kangaroos and wombats, check their pouches for joeys, but in truth, and to our shame, we've not yet reached that point. It's another year or two before we do. We know what we're supposed to do, but in that so-far unlit part of our minds it's still someone else's business. Our failure, and I'm not proud of it. You can be so far in and yet there is always so much farther to go.

In Canberra we check in to a motel and head to Collette and Jim's. There's food (pizza again) and we talk late into the night, about the coming kangaroo cull—the A.C.T. government has set a target figure of 1,600 from the parks and nature reserves around the capital—and Collette's experiences out in the bush at night over the last few winters, protesting and simply trying to keep track of the killing, which the government keeps as secret as possible. She talks about the mass graves, the mutilated corpses they've found—it sounds, as I will later write (and be criticized for the comparison), like Poland, 1942, or Srebrenica in 1995[41]—and then about the absurdities, contradictions, and lies the government has been feeding the public. Even the cull figures are deceptive, she says. The government has sub-licensed the Department of Defence to kill roos on the huge weapons-testing range, just out of town. Another 14,000 kangaroos have been slaughtered there that the government has never talked about. I sit thinking of the fire started last year at the Army firing range, the 58,000 hectares burnt, and don't know what to say. Cats clamber over us as we talk, settle on our laps. The walls are covered with Jim's photographs—roos, wallabies grooming one another, grazing, staring with wide-eyed trust at the camera.

❦

When we get home the next afternoon T. goes straight to the middle gate. Henry and Jonathan, who've been grazing under the peppermint tree, come sidling over, pretending casualness (only pretending: in coming days they'll convey their displeasure at this three-day abandonment). At first Orpheus is nowhere to be seen, but then (no one has eaten him!), hearing T. calling his name, comes pelting up through the scrub and tearing across the field, only—for now the big boys are watching—to stand quietly, disguising his panting, as if nothing has happened and he's hardly noticed she's been away.

41 "Roogate," *The Bungendore Bulletin*, May 2016, and online on various sites.

The Flehmen Response

So much is still a mystery. Tonight I've learnt the name for something we've been noticing since almost the day Henry and Jonathan arrived. The *flehmen response*, sometimes called *flehmening*, or *flehming*. It's found in a large number of mammals—elephants, tigers, buffalo, tapirs, giraffes, goats, horses, sheep—and is marked by those animals drawing back their lips to expose their teeth and gums while inhaling deeply, holding their breath, and assuming a distinctive posture, the head raised as if listening to something a long way off. It can be mistaken for grimacing, laughing, or an expression of aggression (Upper Saxon *flemmen*: to look spiteful), but it's more a matter of sexual communication or detection. It will often occur where an animal of the same species has peed or defecated, and is largely interpreted as the flehmening animal, usually but not always the male, trying to determine whether the conspecific is ready to mate. I'd see Henry doing it up at the top of the paddock overlooking Geoff's flock, and it seemed quite evident he was trying to get a scent of the ewes. But I'd also see him, before he was castrated, following Jonathan about and doing it, head much closer to the ground—or, rather, closer to Jonathan's penis. Often he'd even try to thrust his head into Jonathan's urine stream, as apparently some ungulates will also do, to further test another's sexual readiness, not that I think Jonathan's ever been sexually ready for Henry (but what would I know? apparently homosexuality is quite common among rams, even when there are ewes around).

This inhaling while baring the teeth and gums is to direct pheromone-scented air to the *vomeronasal* organ, a chemosensitive spot located between the palate and the roof of the mouth. I looked it up because, earlier today, T. said that while I'd been up in the house taking a break from hand sawing the railway sleeper she needed cut for the causeway across the swamp (I told you …) so the boys can reach the good grass on the other side without having to struggle through mud, she'd needed the heavy hammer for the star pickets and gone into the cabin to look in the tool cupboard. Pumpkin had followed her and been particularly interested in getting into the writing room. He'd made his own way down there, she said, then didn't want to leave.

After he'd nosed around for a few minutes, nibbling at books and papers—no real damage, apparently, but what would it matter?—he spent a long while closely sniffing the rug before stepping aside, onto the uncovered floorboards, and having a long pee. This brought a smile to my face. All three sheep seem to like taking long pees in my writing room. They only have long pees when they're feeling safe and content, so I take it as a kind of blessing. But then, she said, Pumpkin sniffed his own pee and did "that baring-of-the-teeth, deep-smelling thing."

"What *is* that?" she asked. "Is it normal for them to smell their own pee like that?"

I had no idea whether it was normal or not. Evidently Pumpkin, castrated as he may be, was coming into some sort of precocious sexual maturity. But clearly flehmening is a more nuanced matter than the detection of estrus. If I can deduce a little from the peeing, the close investigation of the rug and the books and papers, the need to get into the room and the reluctance to leave it, *place* may also be involved. Pumpkin, while being hand-reared, spent several quiet hours with me in the writing room while T. was taking Charlie for a walk, or shopping, or had some appointment. I made him a lookout-cum-nest on the broad, low sill of the window looking onto the paddock that at that point he hadn't yet been taken into, and he'd sometimes stand there gazing out, though most often he'd just curl up on the rug and watch me while I wrote.

Was he remembering that today? Experiencing some kind of nostalgia? Paying a visit *back*? Surely it's not just humans for whom memory and desire can become intertwined and confused. Does he dream of his inside self? I'm intrigued that he sniffed the rug so carefully first, and *then* peed. And the flehmen response—intensified, urgent—was that to his *own* pee, or to that of another, *that* other, whom he'd once been?

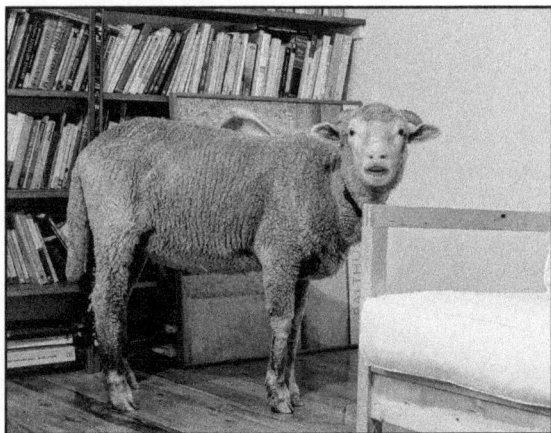

that baring-of-the-teeth, deep-smelling thing

177

Masters of Go

May 2, the coldest day of the year so far, set aside to take Jonathan to the vet to have the cyst in his cheek looked at— T.'s now questioning whether, instead of staking himself on a branch, he might have been bitten by a snake—and what for the last few days, since she announced that it had to happen, I've been calling the Defenestration of the Rat. In truth there's no window involved, unless somewhere in the mind; it's a simple eviction we're talking about,[42] though where this rat is concerned (or rats: we've never been able to ascertain whether

---

42 A part of me does cling to defenestration. There are, for example, the Defenestrations of Prague (1419 and 1618), conducted by Protestants against Catholic officials, in the second of which three chancellors were thrown from a high Town Hall window and miraculously survived, by one account (Catholic) because angels protected them, by another (Protestant) because they'd fallen onto a dung heap, therein starting something of a tradition of Bohemian defenestration, e.g. Jan Masaryk's (murder? suicide?) in 1948 (found below his bathroom window at the Cernin Palace), or that of the novelist Buhomil Hrabal (*Closely Watched Trains*) from a hospital window in 1997, supposedly while feeding pigeons. There's also the self-defenestration of Gilles Deleuze, whose work leans into this book, in Paris on November 4, 1995, lending the concept a philosophical touch. (The house is a metaphor for the mind. Arguably it's myself I'm trying to defenestrate.)

or not he/she acts alone) nothing is ever simple. But first Jonathan, whom we'd thought would be a problem loading into the van but who, tempted by lucerne, is no trouble at all. (Perhaps he *wants* to go to the vet, to get this hurting sorted.)

At the vet's Mark isn't his usual self, is pale, distracted, looks to be in shock. I ask how he's going and he says straight up that overnight his dog has died, in the backyard. They found him this morning. A broken neck, from running into something. Mark is devastated. It must be hard to do anything, carrying a shock like that around, but he gets straight into the van and checks Jonathan's cheek. I don't get in with him, hear him and T. wrestling with Jonathan inside, bangings and thumpings, mutterings of exasperation, and instead look after Charlie who's pacing around the van, afraid something terrible is happening to his friend.

Eventually Mark emerges, heading back into the surgery for needles to do an aspiration. Ten minutes later he gets out of the van again, with blood- and pus-soaked wads of gauze, to show me what was in Jonathan's lump. I go into the surgery with him, to pay and collect some antibiotics. I don't actually see Jonathan front-on until we unload him at home. There's blood all over his left cheek, as if he's been in a fistfight. T. is seething that Mark didn't use an anesthetic. The old farm-animal/pet divide, which she's convinced he can't straddle. I tell her about his dog. She's sorry to hear about that, but emphatic that it doesn't change anything. Of course it doesn't. That's not why I told her.

And now for the eviction. Clearly the rat or rats is/are living behind the tall pantry cupboard. The smell gives them away, and the droppings and other dirt we can see there when we squeeze close enough to the wall and get the torch angle right. I've been hoping all I'll need do is empty the bottom shelf, wrench it from its base, scrub the floor underneath, fill the hole the rat's been coming up through, and re-affix the shelf, but now I see it's not so simple. Everything from the cupboard, all six heavily laden shelves, will have to be unloaded and the doors taken off. Then, with luck, the whole cupboard can be moved aside.

So many things you don't know about a house until you start working on it! And we've only been here twenty months. The work has hardly begun. Relieved of its contents and doors, the cupboard isn't as substantial as it's appeared to be. As we begin to shift it a light-gray rat, large and alone, dashes out in the direction of the kitchen. Somehow I hadn't imagined him to be at home. But that, too, will have to be dealt with later. Underneath the cupboard we find a mess of finely chewed blackened wood pulp gnawed from the surrounding chipboard, three large pieces of which lie amongst the fibers as if marking out the corridors of a rat house. No children, as we'd feared there would be (how could we remove a whole family?), nor any evidence of a hole. Indeed where we'd imagined a masonite floor to be there is solid tile.

The scenario alters immediately. When I clear away the nest, the new story's confirmed. There is no hole at all. This has been a home, a lair, not a point of entry. The rat's been living here alone. It's not been an invasion but a single unwanted guest, and perhaps we're partly responsible. Our careful attempts to keep rats *out* might have meant that at some point he became trapped *in*side. Were there an entrance or exit anywhere, then he would be living with others, or others with him. But I suppose even that's not clear. There were sounds from beneath the pantry cupboard well before I went around the house and sealed off all possible entrances. Even if he hasn't been living there all this time, he's certainly been using it as a larder and hiding place. One piece of evidence aside, I might conclude he's a loner, not so much trapped as living here by choice, but up on the cornice, only reachable, if you're a rat, by standing on top of the pantry cupboard, there's a patch where the paint and paper covering the molded plaster have been clawed away, as if he's been trying to get through to whatever rat family or community lives in the roof space (another thing for later: perhaps that *will* be a defenestration). This scratching, this hole attempt, has only happened in the last week or two, and seems to betoken changed circumstance. It suggests desperation, and I'm sorry about that.

But for now there's work to do. The cupboard must be reinstalled by evening, so the contents, out on the dining table, don't become a feast for the unwanted lodger. We brush-and-pan the nest, scrub the area with disinfectant, then maneuver the cupboard into the kitchen so I can set about attaching a solid base that, once the cupboard is back in place, no rat or mouse will be able to make their way through or under to build a nest again. This done, we right it and return it to the pantry. In one of my earlier attempts to rat-proof the room I wedged a long, thin tube of wire mesh all the way up between the cupboard and wall, only to find the rat using it as a ladder, not in the least deterred by it. I now put it back into place as a temporary measure while we set about finding where the rat is hiding, presumably waiting for the chance to go back to his nest. I know he'll try to use the mesh as a ladder again, so this time I bend the top out and downward, sure he won't be able to get past that. Alternatively I could simply put nothing there, but then there'd be the issue of trying to get him out of where he'd wedge himself, in the dark inner corner between the cupboard and the wall, whereas—this is the plan, anyway—we'll leave the outside door open (the pantry has two doors, one into the kitchen and one out onto the veranda). Surely, if we give him no option, he'll head straight outside when he realizes his nest place is sealed off, and the job will be done.

In fact there's no need to set about finding him. I've been hearing him as I've worked on the cupboard. He's under one of the kitchen benches. All we need do is move it and coax him out. But first, since we want him outside, we erect, across the dining room, a barricade to the rest of the house, leaving the French doors, like the pantry door, open. It's dusk now, and cold outside, but hopefully he'll see his chance to get free of the house and will take it.

We move the bench. At first there seems to be no one there, but he's moving with it. Eventually he makes a break, not through the French doors but back into the pantry and—the first time I've seen him do this, and I'm astonished by the speed—climbs the wire-mesh ladder and, quite undeterred by the bend at the top, is mysteriously, magically, instantaneously on the other side. Almost faster than the eye can see. Not just the climbing, but the appraising and overcoming of the new obstacle. The mind of a rat is lightning fast, I think to myself, and for the moment I'm flummoxed, no match, but then it must seem to him that his life is on the line, and mine isn't. Could *I* think that fast, if it were? Hardly.

By now he's discovered that the base of the cupboard is sealed and he can't get back to his nest. He's nervous, if not actually terrified—again I'm sorry for that—and won't come out for a while. We shift the barrier from the dining room to the inside pantry door, and, to make things easier for rat and human alike, I remove the wire mesh. Hopefully all that's required now is to coax him from behind the cupboard and, since the pantry's outside door is open, see him off into the night. It's autumn, only six o'clock, but already dark outside, a quarter-moon, stars.

Sure enough, just as we finish the new barricade, he breaks again, but this time—for of course he knows his options far better than we—not to the door but into an impossibly small space between the back of the refrigerator and the wall at the other end of the pantry. The back of the refrigerator is entirely sealed but for a finger-hole through which one can reach the re-set mechanism. If he goes in there, which I presume he's done, there'll be no reaching him. He's so frightened that he'll probably be there all evening.

But no, as soon as we dismantle the barricade—declaring a kind of truce for the night—he scampers out from the pantry, across the dining room, down the hall, and into T.'s study. That is, *we* are not quick enough to see him, but Charlie has, and is already in there sniffing about excitedly. We have another chance. There's a second door in the study, out onto the back deck. If we open this and block the door between the hall and study, I should be able to find the rat and, giving him no other option, chase him outside.

We wedge a towel under the hall-side door and open the door to the deck. He's not under the desk, nor behind the cabinets or the first and second bookshelves. I'm beginning to think Charlie was mistaken, but then, moving the last and heaviest bookshelf, I find him, wedged on his side, looking up at me with a red and panicked eye. For a long second we stare at one another, motionless, suspended in time. He thinks he's about to die. But no, I've been in this situation before; history is repeating itself and I'm being given another chance; this time it's different; he won't die, not if I can help it.

There's now only one way out. Confident he'll take it, I pull the bookshelf back from the wall, and he breaks free. Rather than heading out to the deck, however, he runs straight to the hallway door and, despite the towel wedged so firmly under it, finds some way, at the very corner, to push through, and races across the dining room, into the pantry and through the hole in the back of the refrigerator. Gone to ground.

Philip has lent me his copy of Yasunari Kawabata's *The Master of Go,* and I've been reading it for the last few nights. First published in 1954, it's a fictionalized documentary about a game of Go the author covered for a Tokyo newspaper in 1938. The book still has an engaging freshness to it, although, beneath the calm and ritual of Go-Master Shūsai's long last match, it's the anxiety and, on the part of Master and Challenger alike, the almost self-abuse which impress me: the Challenger, at thirty-five, suffers from chronic nervous indigestion and a weak bladder, the Master with a heart condition he'll die from a year later; the match is delayed over and over by the Master's ill health; the Challenger repeatedly and petulantly threatens to quit the game in exasperation. I, too, have a heart condition, though it seems I'm doing better than Go-Master Shūsai.

About the game of Go itself, however, I know nothing, other than—and even this is only an impression—that it's a matter of barricades, forays, one player's attempts to surround the other and prevent them escaping. Tonight, as I read about the Master's taking two hours to make a move, and the Challenger darting out from his barricaded corner, making his own next move in a matter of seconds, I can't help thinking of the rat. It's gone on for months, this tussle of ours, just like the Master's last game. Today I've made another charge and he's held me off again.

There is nothing for it but to call it a night, have dinner, recoup. Neither of us has the inclination to cook. The pizza place in town does a vegan option. We order and, while waiting, re-pack the pantry cupboard. I then go down to the ash garden to retrieve the humane trap, set it up with some peanut butter as bait—supposedly rats find peanut butter irresistible—and a small dish of water lest he get thirsty, and place it by the refrigerator in the pantry. With luck the Challenger will make a false move and we'll be able to relocate him in the morning.

After dinner I go back to the novel, and T. to her thesis. In bed, stirring at 5 a.m., finding me already awake, she tells me she heard something an hour or so before, thinks it was the trap. I lie there a long while trying to work out where to release him. Under the house? By the ash garden where he can join the cabin rats? By the sheep coop where he can join the coop rats? Will they have him? Will he have to do battle? Should I take him farther away? Near any other building in the neighborhood and there's the likelihood of poison—just today, behind the chemist's, I saw a neat, officious-looking "Rodent Bait Station"—and if I take him into the bush there are owls, foxes, feral cats.

But in the morning, of course, the trap's empty, the door still open, the peanut butter untouched in its little dish. He hasn't been so stupid, or perhaps it's just not very good peanut butter. There are a few small pieces of Charlie's dry food between the entrance to the humane trap and the refrigerator. At first I take these as a sign both that he's been active during the night, and that he has a sense of humor, is thumbing his nose at us—it must have been *he* who was communicating in tomato-code!—but T. tells me she put these there just before coming to bed, to try to entice him to the trap. Clearly the rat has been living on Charlie's leftovers and water while trapped. If anything, that these few pieces are still there is a sign the rat hasn't been. Perhaps he hasn't come out at all. Still petrified. I feel sorry again.

For the next few days we have other things to do. A breathing space in which to plan our next move. For a second night we leave the trap by the refrigerator, and for a second morning find it untouched. Perhaps he's not in the refrigerator base at all. T. thinks he's back under the kitchen bench. That evening I sit nearby, at the dining table, reading the last of the Kawabata; and, yes, once or twice, very faintly, a sound comes from under there. In the novel, at White 130, Master Shūsai has made a false move, and from there on knows that he's lost. Observers and commentators say the young Challenger has set him up with a piece of modern trickery that's out of the spirit of the game, as if his determination to win has led him to violate an ancient aesthetic. It's a new age that's defeating the Master, they say. I wouldn't be surprised if the Master hasn't made the false move deliberately, as a means of throwing the match, to get out of what might seem to him a kind of moral dilemma.

The third day then, and time for a concerted attempt at an endgame. We've planned carefully. Around midday we clear the dining table and tip it onto its side. Placed across the room it will block off the rest of the house almost entirely. Across the space remaining we place one of T.'s paintings, of angel-like figures falling into what I've always imagined as Hell, though she herself never interprets, and across the pantry door space we wedge a large pastry board, to seal that option entirely. The rat has no way free except through the open French doors. We then begin to move the kitchen bench, pivoting it on one of its legs. Ten centimeters, twenty, thirty, fifty, and suddenly—just as we're thinking he mightn't be there—he dashes out, runs straight to the inner corner of the upturned dining table but, finding the gap between that and the wall too narrow even for him, runs along the table's base to the painting, along the edge of the falling angels ("Go!" I am thinking, "Go!"), and, almost unbelievably, out onto the veranda. For several seconds all we can do is stare, but then snap to and close the doors firmly. Gone! After all this time! Gone!

But then, straight away, anticlimax, and something like guilt. It feels like a victory, but also selfish, a kind of thuggery. How much chance did he stand, really? What have we done other than assert our territory, reaffirmed the species barrier we spend so much time arguing against? If the house, actual and experienced, has its parallel in the house of the mind, and the house of ideas that the mind itself lives in, then in throwing out the rat we have also thrown out the *idea* of the rat, the idea that the rat *was* or still *is*, what it might *be*. An idea that had got into our minds and was gnawing at us, unsettling us. Is that what we've tried to do? Of course not. We are "animal rights" people, "animal *advocates*." Or so we like to tell ourselves. But how far have we come, really, if we can't live with a rat?

We set the house back to rights. I go down to work in the cabin; T. takes the sheep into the ragged autumn garden to graze amongst the spent vegetables, a treat for them and a good start to the winter cleanup. There's a bit of golden late-afternoon sun before a breeze picks up and the chill rises. A half hour of dusk, cockatoo-filled, before dark. Coming back to the house a little later, treading carefully over the pitch-black lawn, I wonder how the rat will fare without the central heating. I say as much to T. and she tells me she thinks he's sheltering under the big wooden box at the street-end of the veranda. In guilt and pity I take the little dish of untouched peanut butter from the humane trap, top it with some of the seeds we keep for the sheep, and go back out into the chill to leave it by the box, smiling when I find she's already given him a water bowl.

The next morning, when I check it, the dish is licked clean. Not a seed to be seen.

Codas

We've been overseas, visiting T.'s parents again. My sister—she of the snakes, and without whose help we could never think of such trips—has been looking after the farm and the boys in our absence, and Charlie's been consoling himself in the company of Seca, her young bull-mastiff cross, whom Charlie's known since he, Seca, was a pup. You wouldn't think, to look at them, that Charlie was the mentor, or Seca (five times his size) the protégé.

But now we're home. My sister is back in her own house at the foot of the range, having weathered a mountain August full of rain. The sheep are out in the sun after a month cooped up, unable to get to their favorite grazing place because the swamp had turned into a lake, covering the causeway T.'s so lovingly restored. My beautiful writing room has mold all along one of the cornices because somewhere or another the roof of the cabin has leaked, but I'll deal with that shortly; eventually there'll have to be a new roof. And Orpheus Pumpkin has lost one of his horns. We don't know how it happened. Perhaps a butting contest with one of the others, though more likely he got it caught on something. We joke that he's now a unicorn, but it can't have been any laughing matter. I can't imagine how much it must have hurt. My sister says that, on the day he lost it, he came up from the swamp with blood streaming down the side of his head. But of course, prey-creature that he is, he'd have been silent throughout. Thankfully a new horn seems to be growing. Indeed, overall he's growing so much that, some mornings, in the mist, it's hard to tell him from the others. All three, with their heavy winter wool, are almost ready for shearing.

All three, too, were angry with us for going away, though forgave us after the second day, or seemed to, bribed with apples. Now, as T. is digging holes and planting a long row of pine seedlings along the southern fence to shield us from our new neighbors (two long-empty houses on West Street sold while we were away), they hardly ever leave her side. Her joy in coming back to them is palpable. It's as if, after a winter away, spring has come to her, too. She spends an hour each evening, just before dusk, down in the paddock with the poop-scooper and wheelbarrow, scraping up their droppings (piled in the compost corner they become an amazing worm farm, a wonderful resource for the garden beds), although much of the time, when I look over to her, she's crouched with them, talking, or trying to control Pumpkin, who has a spring fever and, one-horned as he is, loves to butt anything and everything, especially the wheelbarrow.

It's not as if we weren't busy over there. T.'s grandmother died, and there was all the business of the funeral, the masses. T. wrote a difficult article, on animal grief, as a test-run for part of her thesis. I had my own writing to do, and there were, as always, animals. The cat, Bianca, and a new dog, Pika, scarcely more than a pup, whom T.'s parents have taken in because they've missed Bobbi so much, and with each of whom we've developed a particular bond. Now it'll be they who miss us. I joke that T.'s like a double Persephone, gone in each hemisphere when the weather cools. There were rescues as well—a ram, a rooster, an injured pig—and helping a friend set up a new sanctuary, and other work with the small, tight network of animal rescuers we're part of there. There is no end to care.

Summer is still two months off, but already there's talk of another dangerous bushfire season. The papers I left on the writing room desk are curled from the water leak, the ink on them blurred and faded; three of my notebooks have had their top edges soaked and are bent and damp and will have to be dried, aired, and put into my old book-binder's press to be flattened again. There's the van to get back on the road after a failed animal rescue while we were away, and seeds and seedlings to pot, garden beds to prepare, accumulated bills to pay. While I've been making a start I've been thinking of the same time last year. Another week, and it'll be October. Pumpkin was born on October 4 and came to us on the 14th—perhaps there should be a birthday party!—and by that time the cicadas had begun to appear, and there'd been the tragedy of the ducklings. The ducks have been around again this year but fewer of them and no ducklings yet, though with last year in mind we've kept the pool brimming, and T. has checked and repaired the little ladder she made for them, adding stepping stones to make it even easier for them to get out of the water. I've been thinking that this, the absence of ducklings, is perhaps because the weather has been slower to warm this year, and they've not hatched yet, or that brooding pairs, conscious of what happened last year, have been giving our pond a wide berth—that maybe they've decided to conduct their swimming lessons in the swamp instead.

And there have, of course, been the boys to settle and re-habituate after our absence. The apples have broken the ice, but there's still distance. T.'s been working hard at it and chiding that I haven't been doing enough. In the last two days, the warmest so far—the temperature almost up to 20!—she's taken her computer into the paddock and sat there reading while they grazed. A couple of days ago I went to sit with them, in the light breeze and the sunshine. The boys were grazing in a kind of rhythm, moving slowly away, coming back, moving away again. I watched their mouths as they tore at the grass, saw that this was rhythmical as well, two tears up and outward, one back, two outward, one back, like a barber a bit drowsy after lunch, cutting on remote control. I thought it was just Jonathan, but then saw Henry doing it too, and Pumpkin, each with their slightly different rhythm, but rhythm nonetheless. Herd music! While I was watching them Pumpkin came over to T., pretending at first he didn't like to be scratched—his wool is so thick!—but then getting down on his knees, settling beside her, ruminating, as if he'd let go of something, relaxed into gift, for suddenly that seems the word, *gift*, without givers, not him to her, or her to him, just the *space* of it, the space of gift. And it, this something, this gift thing, settled over us for a while. Even Charlie, who can get so possessive when anyone comes close to T., seemed to feel it, lying there quietly, gazing out.

That evening we were speaking of Jonathan, and T. asked what I thought it might be that has changed in him, to make him so much calmer and more approachable. Even with his clear annoyance about our absence, there's almost none of his once-relentless bleating at the gate. I said it might just be they've all settled into the place a bit more. Probably her causeway mending, just before we left, had helped. They'd not been able to go down to the lush bottom grass during the August rains, that's true, but now that the weather was warmer and drier they'd been going up and down two or three times a day and seemed to be relishing the freedom and extra territory. But who knows? Jonathan's a bit of a mystery. A mystery amongst mysteries.

We went to bed around midnight, slept well. I woke at seven and lay there listening to the cockatoos thumping around on the tin roof over the deck beside the bedroom. They must have then come down onto the railing because the clatter ceased and instead there was a range of softer sounds, from jagged squawks to quieter raspings, chirps, squeaks, mutterings, intakes of breath. A whole conversation. I thought of the woman in the U.S. with whom T.'s been in correspondence, who records bird sounds and then slows them down to reveal the complex patterns within them, and wondered what she'd make of these. A little later I got up and, waiting for the coffee to rise, was watching two cockatoos on the deck rail, thinking they must be friends, or a pair, when a third joined them and began clambering precariously about the vertical struts, as if on a jungle gym. A kid? Theirs? It's spring, after all. Then, with my coffee, at the dining table, sitting down to write my diary, I was distracted by another pair, at the birdbath in the herb garden, who seemed almost to be kissing one another—perhaps a behaviorist would say *grooming*—and then saw a third fly up to join them and realized that these were a family also.

I finished my coffee. T. wasn't up yet. Remembering something else we'd been talking about—there's an old concrete slab just below the coop we've been thinking of putting a small shelter on—I went down there to take measurements. The boys *baa*ed greetings with their mouths full and went back to their grazing. By the time I'd finished, five or six minutes later, they'd munched their way across and were standing in a half circle about me. I went over and rubbed Henry's neck and talked to him quietly about how nice a morning it was. He started to pee, that unmistakable sign of contentment. I looked over and saw Jonathan begin to pee also, and then Pumpkin. Gift again. When I got back to the house, T. was up and standing at the kitchen window. "Babies!" she called as I came in. "Babies!"

And they were there. Ducklings. The breeding pair—

was it last year's?—and a brood, passing through the shadow under the peppermint gum, so tumultuously it was hard to tell how many. Heading for the pond but turning away at the last second. Last year's couple then? Being more careful? I looked at the water level in the pond, two or three centimeters below the brim—would that be safe enough?—and determined to top it up as soon as the way was clear. But almost before I'd finished my sigh of relief at their newfound common sense they turned back, headed directly for the pond, and were in, a tumble of tiny bodies, how many still impossible to tell. We watched from the kitchen window, breath bated, ready to intervene. Some of the ducklings were off around the rim— no problems with swimming!—and others were watching the mother get in, clamber out again, get in, clamber out, to show them how it was done. Then first one, then another, were up and out, another, then another, and now, back from their excursion around the rim, several more, clambering up over the stepping stones, or hopping up the ladder bridge, six, seven, *eight* of them, then in again, out again. So, lessons *can* be learnt, at least by them. Let's hope we can do likewise.

❧

Thought has difficulty negotiating the rough terrain of reality. I once would have tried very hard to paper over the ridges and gullies of it. Now I'm not so inclined. It's not that I think we should stop thinking—hardly! (though I do remember, often, the line from Blanchot's *Thomas the Obscure*, "I think therefore I am not") and it would of course be impossible— but that we should be aware of our propensity to push thought to premature solutions. Approaching non-human animals, especially, we have to be very careful, mistrusting, suspicious of the ability of thought alone to see and resolve things, by which I don't just mean—though I do also mean—the way the opening to animals in the first place seems to have to be a "heart"-driven rather than thought-driven matter (it's also a *place*-driven matter, T. says over my shoulder). How would thought get us there, really, when for so many thousands of years it has established patterns—not just stream- and riverbeds, but a whole terrain—to help ensure that we *repress* the animal? Perhaps, in the long run, thought *is* all we have (T. demurs) but we must be so careful, so attentive to its whispers and glimpses, to burrs on the edge of the mind. We may never break from the cage of it, into some hypothetical Open, but perhaps we can expand that cage a bit, make it less of a liability to the world around us.

That's the thing about living with non-human animals: no complacency; absolute unpredictability. T. seems to be developing her own preoccupation with roosters. Perhaps it began with the rooster we rescued while we were away. Now a friend has put out a general call for a home for an abused rooster she's been made aware of, and T.'s been helping her search. They've found a place with Paula, another friend, who has a beloved rooster, Andrew, and is happy to take on a second. She's been keeping the new rooster, Bullet, in a separate area from Andrew while she gets to know him. Just this morning we've heard that, overnight, Bullet has somehow got out of this separate area and into Andrew's cage and killed him. Paula thinks Bullet must have been raised as a fighting cock. She's distraught. Now that he's killed Andrew she can't bear to look at him. A tragedy. But who could have anticipated it? Inexperience. Miscalculation. You think you've solved something and it explodes in your face.

Cages, and cages as metaphor. But that's not what I wanted to write about here. I've been thinking instead of the coats, to write about which I have first to tell about the shearing. A joyous thing, in some ways—but also fraught.

ℨ

For Pumpkin's birthday we bought a watermelon. Jonathan, Henry, and Charlie loved it, but Pumpkin wasn't so interested, only started to join the feast when I brought out a half-loaf of fresh-baked bread. As we squatted amongst the crusts and melon rinds the sun was hot on our shoulders, the second day that week over 25 degrees. The boys were visibly uncomfortable under their heavy fleeces, panting, and we called Mick the shearer. He's based at Borowa, almost three hundred kilometers away, but he and his wife Nolene do a spring round. He said they'd be passing through on the 28th.

On the night of the 27th they stayed somewhere nearby, with friends. We were their first stop, and so also the place where Mick discovered he'd brought the wrong handle for the shears. A lot of swearing and a few fruitless phone calls later he'd managed—bush mechanics!—to rig something up and we got under way. They had two recently shorn ewes in a cage on the back of their ute, on their way down to a sanctuary on the city outskirts, and the boys couldn't take their eyes off them, a point I mention only because it made it so much easier to corral all three—Jonathan, Henry, and Pumpkin—in the coop, where they could be shorn without anyone doing a runner. Last year, with too fresh a memory of his castration, Henry had struggled, and received some unpleasant nicks from the shears, gentle as Mick tried to be, so we decided this time to begin with Jonathan, who we thought would be calmer and less likely to frighten Pumpkin. He'd watched Henry and Jonathan being shorn the year before, but he was only three weeks old then and probably had little memory of it, let alone any sense of it as something that might happen to him.

It worked. Jonathan seemed glad to be being relieved of his fleece. As the wool began to peel off in arc by sweeping arc, Pumpkin, from two meters away, stood in wide-eyed fascination. When Jonathan was finished, he went over to sniff at the fleece and practically lay down of his own accord, awaiting his turn. I think both T. and I gasped as the shears went around his remaining horn, which until this had barely peeped from his thick curls but now stood out in eleven-centimeter glory. He was so *thin* suddenly, a lamb again. Then Henry, less trouble than the year before, though—veteran of four or five shearings by now—he also landed two or three well-aimed kicks near Mick's groin, as if to indicate his submission was anything but voluntary.

And then suddenly, I don't know … there was *strangeness*. An already bright morning was almost too bright. The boys were so much *lighter*, so *naked*, and clearly felt it themselves. They looked at each other in a kind of awe, and almost tiptoed over the spring grass, as if even it were more fragile, more delicate than it had been. I thought of the wonder of a first snowfall. For Pumpkin especially, although I think for him there was also, very quickly, sadness, as if something had been taken from him that, for all he knew, he would never get back.

After three more warm days, however, and nights that, with all the extra straw we gave them to compensate, were perhaps not too cold, the weather closed in. The day's maximum dropped by ten degrees and the night's minimum by almost as much. When Henry and Jonathan first came to us they'd just been shorn and the weather closed in in the same way. Back then, after three days of rain and cold, Henry, a pure Merino and more delicate than Jonathan's mixed breed, had developed pneumonia. For most of his first two weeks with us we were giving him daily antibiotic injections. We all got used to it, and he got better quickly, but it was an awkward way to start. Fearing a repeat of this, T. had already been thinking of coats, checking all the likely places in the area—the supermarkets, the secondhand shops, the produce stores, even the chic pet boutique at Sublime Point—for something she could put on the boys' backs to keep them warm.

A woman at the department store said she'd seen some large-dog weather shields at a place at the foot of the mountains. We made a special trip down and were in luck, found weather jackets in just the right sizes: XXLs for Henry and Jonathan, an L for Pumpkin. Charlie already had his own (an S/M) and wore it often in such weather. The colors of these new coats were a bit garish—red, blue, gray, and white horizontal stripes—but beggars can't be choosers. We drove back feeling pleased with ourselves. It was already late afternoon, drizzling and cold. T. immediately went down into the paddock to put them on.

It was harder than we could ever have imagined. With Pumpkin not so much so, but then, given his age and mixed upbringing, his tolerance for new things is higher than the others'. He let T. put his coat on him without a fuss, but the moment she did so, the others, who'd been standing by watching, backed off ten meters or more, as if something alarming had just happened. When Pumpkin tried to follow them they stamped their feet at him in warning. He was confused, hurt—his friends suddenly treating him as an enemy!—but T. comforted him and tried to coax him to eat some of the fresh lucerne she'd brought in order to distract them. Pumpkin started to eat and as he did so Jonathan, always tempted by food, came over as if trying to work out who this new creature was, but when Pumpkin turned to him ("It's me!"), he bolted to the far side of the paddock. T. went after him but he wouldn't let her near. She came up to the house to think about it—leaving the boys in their standoff—and went back down with one of the coats on her own back, like a shawl, thinking this might habituate them a little. But, far from it, whatever had pounced upon Pumpkin and seemed to be devouring him—was this a primeval memory of jaguars, mountain lions?—had now attacked her!

At last she managed to corner Jonathan. He had his back to the bottom fence and seemed paralyzed with fear, but T. on her own side was just as afraid of losing one of them to pneumonia, and convinced that, once the coats were on, the warmth the boys would feel would make them understand. She managed to get a coat onto him, but before she got the second strap fastened he'd got away, raced back towards Pumpkin's old cubby, and begun running recklessly around and around it in a way that (for, hearing T.'s cries of exasperation, I'd come down to the paddock) gave me the distinct and alarming impression he was losing his mind, though evidently he was just—desperately—trying to get this something off his back. At last he came to rest in a corner by the northern fence, cowed, head bowed, as if he expected to be slaughtered at any moment. T. threw her own coat off and went to him, managed to get his coat off also. But where was Henry in all this? We turned to see him across from us on the other side of the paddock. When T. went over to him it was to find him scratched and bleeding in a way that could only suggest that, while our back had been turned in our alarm at Jonathan's frenzy, he had tried, in his own, to escape over the fence.

And then suddenly nothing. Quiet. Jonathan's coat was off, Pumpkin's coat was off, T.'s coat was off, I had spirited the offending articles away, and all five of them—T., Jonathan, Henry, Pumpkin, Charlie—were huddled in the middle of the paddock, as if checking out each other's parts, to make sure they were whole, and safe, after such a terrible visitation.

Up in the house our postmortem went on for an hour. Evidently we'd done something stupid, again, but what *was* it? We'd only narrowly avoided a tragedy. What *had* that been about? Our motives had been the very best: who could have thought that slipping coats on their backs, to keep them warm, could be such a terrifying thing? But clearly we had become in their eyes—or had introduced, or been suddenly attacked by—a predator. Either that or—bearing in mind the milder reaction, at first, to the apparition of Pumpkin's coat—they had encountered, as it overtook him, then T., and then, in T.'s guise, attached itself to Jonathan, something so inexplicable that their mind could react in no other way than panic.[43]

Now, thankfully, the nights have warmed a little, but what will we do next year? Try to delay the shearing? Paint the coats a sheep color and try again to get the boys to accept them? Attach some of their own wool to them, so that it might seem as if we're trying to give them back to themselves? Every explanation, every possibility, seems a groping, over a terrain that's become rough and uncertain again. And the boys, what were *they* talking about, down there, huddled in the coop?

※

You have to end somewhere. Or pause. On the threshold. Letting one thing go so another can start. It's a month later. T. has found Pumpkin's horn in the swamp grass down by the bottom fence, so we figure he must have got it caught in the wire and wrenched it off to get free. The ants have thoroughly cleaned it. She wants to bore holes in the sides so she can string it and wear it about her neck on special occasions. And a fourth sheep has joined us. Jason, a black sheep, which is to say very dark brown, found six weeks ago in a swampy brickyard southwest of Sydney with rotting feet. We've had

---

43 Although I've been unable to find such a thing on any list of phobias I've read so far (but then, of course, such lists have been drawn up by humans), clearly sheep have a fear of stripes, a fear that seems greater the more brightly colored they are.

Codas

him for three weeks, in quarantine, while we've treated them—the boys visiting him each day to talk through the fence—and his hooves have improved dramatically. The vets told us we can let him into the paddock with the others, and he's been there since morning. The plan was to re-home him but one day, working at the edge of the vegetable garden, I felt his warm breath on my neck—I was close to the quarantine-yard railings—and realized that we had to keep him.

It's dusk. Deep dusk. Almost night. We're preparing a spinach and tofu curry, a vegan version of *palak paneer*, and talking as we do so, going over events of the day, Jason's joy at his new friends, their ease with him, the duckling count (eleven!), the need to finish repairing the boys' causeway this year, the ferns which have at last appeared from under the lid of the yellow piano. As if on an inspiration—who knows what he's been thinking, lying there on the rug in the middle of the kitchen, *doggedly* under foot?—Charlie gets up, heads straight to his dog door, pads down the steps onto the dark lawn and crosses to the paddock gate, goes through his private entrance, and says hello. We watch him from the window, the kitchen light turned off so we can see better. We see him bobbing about between them—Henry, Pumpkin, Jonathan, Jason— and lose him for a second, find him, lose him again, but no, there he is, his small white body, neck craned upward, now licking Henry's face, now Jonathan's, now Pumpkin's, now Jason's, his tail wagging like a pale wand, they standing there so calmly, heads bowed, receiving. I wouldn't be surprised if all five were having a pee.

201

Thanks and Acknowledgments

First and foremost to Teya Brooks Pribac, without whom this book would not have been conceived, let alone written. Then, for their contributions and encouragements, to John Kinsella, to my sister Zoie, and to Alison Moore, Jason Grossman, Melissa Boyde, Vicki Wilson, Kate Livett, Sy Woon, Tim Curnow, Chris and Jeremy Townend, Andras Berkes-Brandl, Veronica Sumegi, and Yuya Toyozumi. Parts of this book were drafted while I was the 2015–16 Australia Council Fellow in Fiction, and in my capacity as Honorary Associate Professor in Australian Literature at the University of Sydney. I wish to express my very real gratitude to those institutions. A version of Chapter 9 ("Herd Music") was published in *Southerly* 76.1 (2016). A version of Chapter 10 ("Interlude") was published in the anthology *After Coetzee*, edited by A. Marie Hauser (Faunary Press, 2017).

About the Author

David G. Brooks is a poet, novelist, short-fiction writer, and essayist. He has taught literature at various Australian universities, and from 1999 until 2018 was co-editor of *Southerly*, the premier journal of Australian literature and new Australian writing. His work has been widely anthologized and translated, and has won or been shortlisted for numerous awards (the National Book Award; the NSW, WA, and Queensland Premiers' Awards; the Adelaide Festival Award; and an Australia Council Fellowship for his distinguished contribution to Australian and international literature, among others). His novel *The Fern Tattoo* was shortlisted for the Miles Franklin award, and the *Sydney Morning Herald*—which called Brooks "one of Australia's most skilled, unusual and versatile writers"—described his poetry collection *The Balcony* as "an electric experience." Currently honorary associate professor in Australian literature at the University of Sydney, Brooks is a vegan and animal rights advocate, and lives in the Blue Mountains of New South Wales.

www.ingramcontent.com/pod-product-compliance
Lightning Source LLC
Chambersburg PA
CBHW031507270326
41930CB00006B/299